Just Once

Rhonda Lucas

Trilogy Christian Publishers
A Wholly Owned Subsidiary of Trinity Broadcasting Network
2442 Michelle Drive, Tustin, CA 92780

10 9 8 7 6 5 4 3 2 1

Library of Congress Cataloging-in-Publication Data is available.

ISBN 978-1-64773-626-2

ISBN 978-1-64773-627-9 (eBook)

Dedication

Where do I begin when it comes to dedicating this book?

I will start with the beginning of my journey. It is to my mom, my prayer warrior, the one who brought life to me on October 3, 1967, and taught me to live when life brings death and find hope in the midst. I love you.

My Matt, my best friend in marriage for almost thirty-one years. I know God joined us together; there is no one on this earth who makes me laugh as you do. I trust your love, your love for Jesus and your family. I will never forget the picture in my mind as you lay flat on your face on the grave of our son, as you wept before God to give us strength. You haven't wavered for one moment; you continue to give all glory to God; you walk with a brokenness that's beautiful.

My girl Sharon Mackenzie, my only girl, I am honored to have had the privilege to raise you. You carry poise, grace, and compassion. You've allowed this sorrow to build and strengthen character in you. I love you…

My baby boy, Micah Seth, you were born strong, you remain strong. You completed us, you have brought peace, joy, and our hearts are full of gratitude for who you are. Never ever stop hugging me. I love you…

My family all over this world, I thank you. When you received the sad news you were here, you know what role you've played in our journey, and I am forever grateful. I never wanted you to have to share this pain with me, but you stepped in and helped to carry the sorrow. Forever grateful.

My friends, the ones who call and ask how I am, who wept with me and for me, and still continue to do so, Thank you.

Caleb's Cup Visionaries, Joe Fitzpatrick, and Ben Houston, you had the vision to see Caleb's message of who he was live on, and because of you both, we have spread hope. You believed for us when we were not strong enough.

Casey Houston and Veronica, thank you for believing in the vision for women to gather "A Time for us" together and share our stories, laugh, pray, and become a community.

And last, but not least: to my moms who have lost a piece of your heart that can't be replaced with new memories and pictures, to the moms whom I can look in your eyes and see the tears that others cannot see. I walk with you. I weep with you. I rejoice with you. I hope with you. You may not know me personally, but if you've lost a child in many ways' we know each other better than most. We can stand together with hope knowing one day we will hold them again, they will hug us, and we will hear the words, "Mom, I love you". Until then, we will pray, and we will find laughter, joy, celebrations, and love as never before, and give yourself credit for you are living out the hardest job on earth, living without your child.

And my faithful God, I end with You not because You are last but because You are the beginning and the end. I know I couldn't in any way, shape, or form be where I am right now had it not been for the grace You have given me over and over again. I couldn't sleep if I didn't have the blanket of Your comfort over me, I couldn't have hope for tomorrow if I didn't experience Your new mercies every morning. I believe You've wiped my tears in the midnight hours, You've held me when I didn't have the strength to stand. I Love You, Jesus.

Caleb, I will hold you again, forever, not Just Once.

Table of Contents

Forward

What an honor to be able to write the forward for *Just Once*. It is a book we have had to live out as the husband of Rhonda and father of Caleb; it couldn't be any closer to my heart.

You will read this book and hear from the heart of Rhonda as she navigates the most painful thing she has ever encountered—losing her first-born son Caleb.

From the absolute shock of finding out her son is no longer with us to seeing God's hand of mercy and grace all over her. How does one deal with this kind of pain? I watched my wife as she shared and wrote it out early in this journey, and by sharing how we must "find purpose in the pain".

This statement has driven her to be completely transparent about Caleb's death. She has been willing to share every detail so that maybe one person would hear her and that they would not make the same mistake Caleb made. The best part of this book is her vulnerability, and I believe this is why people are listening. People are seeking to find the truth and searching for what is real.

So, if this is you, find a comfortable spot and grab some tissues, and take this journey with Rhonda as she shows you that God is greater than any situation or problem. He is not offended by your tough questions.

Just Once will help you find that there is no substitute for Jesus. He is the answer, solution, cure, and antidote for all your pain and problems. He is with you always, and in her worst and most devastating moments was when she pressed into Him like never before.

Caleb, we love you. We miss you. We grieve for you, but not without HOPE. For the day will come again… indeed it will.

Just Once

I felt it for months; the title came quickly because over and over, I would say to myself, "Just Once." However, the courage, I guess you could say to start writing this raw, painful, bittersweet story, has been tough. I would start to write over and over again, get through a page, and then the pain would be so strong that I had to stop. This wasn't an easy write. I have had to physically, emotionally, and spiritually live out this book. But we know that nothing that is birthed is easy, and that is where my story will begin.

I was born in New York, and I knew the brutal winters of New York and the hot summers until the age of ten. The first house I remember so vividly was this cute little yellow house, very quaint, almost like a storybook home. The strangest thing was, it was right across the street from a drive-in theater. These were a big deal back when I was young, and I remember looking out our front window and being able to watch the movie for free, basically. It was kind of a cool thing, and I don't think I would really enjoy it now for fear of what would show on the screen.

We soon were able to live in another home that my dad loved so much. The last home we lived in before we moved to Georgia was on 103 acres up on a hill. It was a blue house with windows and a porch that extended the whole length of the home. My parents were pastors of a church nestled in a little town of Hornell, NY, a small quaint little town. Our church looked like one out of a movie, the tall cathedral, the older pews, and yet it was beautiful and magical to me. You could walk out, and two steps to the right was a Kentucky Fried Chicken (KFC) in the city of Hornell, New York, and let me tell you back then, that was the Chick-Fil-A of today, and it smelled so good. My childhood memories of running across the street after church and getting a choc- olate pudding and a drumstick still make my mouth water and bring joy to me.

I remember Sundays meant long days of church in the morning, eating, and going back for the Sunday night service and many times falling asleep on the pews; these were the old school pews with no padding and cold. There weren't padded seats and fancy lights during worship. I remember the Wednesday night services and all the events we had to go to. I remember many times sitting at hospitals while my parents visited the sick. There was something so very special about those days. I saw my parents work hard to be there for everyone; little did I know I was taking it all in, and it would one day become a part of my character. I can't say I was always jumping for joy to have no choice to be there all the time; many times, I didn't want to get in the car and sit for hours at a stranger's home while they talked about Jesus the whole time. I just wanted to stay home and watch Happy Days.

When I was at home, I was outside most of the time. I was a Girl Scout and took piano lessons. We had farms, and I mean the real deal next to us, and we would get to milk the cows. Back then, this was how you got your milk. I had never heard of almond milk, cashew milk; it was downright 100 percent cows. There were chickens that I got to feed. I wasn't the flawless pretty little girl; I had a lot of tomboy in me with a mixture of princess, and how I loved it all. I had some seriously bad haircuts; a mullet with bangs wasn't winning me any pageant titles.

We would roam the acres and acres of land, see deer everywhere, and when winters hit, it was snow, snow, and snow. So much snow that the schools didn't close down very often because this was a way of life for our city, even the principal who lived close by made sure we were at school and several times picked us up.

My parents were loved by so many in the town, but soon another position for a church in Decatur, Georgia, opened for my dad, and he felt it was time for a new journey. We were used to moving as we traveled in a motorhome for many years, going from church to church. We were called The Singing Parsons. I had learned at a young age to not hold too tightly to anything. I didn't feel insecure; I was just used to letting go. The great thing I felt that when I was young was that the transition of moving was so much easier to making friends and getting involved in new activities, especially back then. I am grateful there were no social media to compare what was better and who my old friends had replaced for me. There were no social media to show me birthday parties and celebrations that I was no longer invited to. I think it was a good thing for this traveling girl.

Isn't it crazy how there are certain things that stand out so clearly in your mind, and maybe they weren't even the most important? I remember this transition well, our Old English Sheepdog in the moving van with my dad and brother. In the small car, it was my mom, Gina, and I barely able to move, a long drive to this place called Georgia and not one electronic or DVD player, just books to read.

We made it. I will never forget the day of pulling in on 200 Deer Run Road, Ellenwood, Georgia. I even remember the zip code. I was so excited to see our brand new cedar home, a huge oak tree in the front yard, a huge, flat yard of three acres, not many compared to what I was used to, but I could ride my bike in my driveway, it was flat and long, and everything was brand new. I was so happy. I remember how I felt the anticipation of walking into the home and smelling the brand new smell of the carpet, fresh and newly painted wood. For the first time, I was going to live in something new and not on wheels, a secure, beautiful home. I ran quickly to see the bedroom Gina and I would share. It was the coolest room, a desk built into the corner of the room with a window, arched ceilings, and a walk-in closet. I didn't care at that time that I had to share a room; she was my buddy anyway, and I loved watching over her.

My mom had ordered a Holly Hobby bedspread; it wasn't babyish; it was cool and the latest craze. Try to remember we didn't mature as kids do now. I played with baby dolls for years; maybe that's why I wanted to be a mom so bad; I felt I had so much practice. I was an expert at Baby Alive and No More Tears; I knew how to change a fake baby doll's diaper faster than anyone. If there was a new baby doll out at stores that could do anything, it was on my wish list. I wasn't too much into Barbie dolls; maybe they seemed to perfect, and I didn't feel motherly when I played with them. I know I am not popular because of that; all those little, tiny pieces just seemed to stress me out. Funny thing, my daughter never liked them either, but boy, she loved her baby dolls.

Those years truly are priceless years; I think I reflect more on them now than I ever did before. They are years full of building blocks, stumbling blocks, and memories of innocence and youth. I have so many memories of the smell of school buses, some good, some bad, memories of cafeteria food that looked like porridge. Nothing was perfect but yet felt so right. I remember my first real crush and sitting by him on the school bus. I had a cold, and snot was running down my face; I was mortified, and there weren't any Kleenex in the cute little packages we have now lying around. Why would he want to talk when I wanted to hide and run? Finally, I had no choice, I just used my sleeve, and for some reason, the snot went even further across my cheek. I find it so strange the things that we remember, I think because I felt so embarrassed and I didn't want to be his girlfriend anymore because I felt when he saw me, he saw me wiping my nose on my sleeve. Again, the things we remember as a child that may have left memories that embarrassed us or maybe even left a tiny scar you can't see with the naked eye.

Just that memory alone reminds me that we should be careful of the things we say to children because you never know they could already be battling insecurity from a runny nose that day.

Oh, the memories I have of childhood are kind of funny when looking back. I think my first kiss was when I was playing spin the bottle. Did anyone play that game and feel as dumb as I did? I can't say we would actually kiss when we played, it was the fastest peck on the lips or cheek ever, but boy, that was the game you played back then. Maybe you are old enough to remember the game Seven Minutes in Heaven; it was anything but heaven. Just basically two preteens with maybe some acne and teeth that needed to be brushed. We would stand and stare at each other until our seven minutes were up and make our friends think it was spent kissing. It actually should have been called seven minutes in a nightmare. Probably not one of us cared that we had Cheetos in

RHONDA LUCAS

our teeth or smeared across our face, then the colored rubber bands popping off. This was plain innocent fun, and that it was.

Friends were easy to have at that time, and that age seemed easy to me, a little talk over lunch or recess, and we were the best of friends. Isn't it funny how back then, a friend would say do you want to come home with me after school? And it was like "sure," no questions asked, and now I won't even go home with someone I have known for months. I kind of miss the innocence of those days when you didn't have to show your license, birth certificate, and credit check to go home with a friend.

It was our childhood, and in a way, our trust wasn't broken yet, at least for me. Now, I am aware not everyone has had a good childhood; I am aware that many were abused emotionally, sexually, and verbally, so I don't dismiss that at all. My heart breaks for children and adults whose childhood was stolen from them. I feel we need to be so aware if we ever sense children going through something that is taking away their innocence; abuse of any kind is not acceptable.

I loved my life, pretty cool being the preacher's kid and having this cool house with the oak tree and the swing on it; I was proud of my life. Simple life, but good. It wasn't too long, though, before I felt my world starting to change. I sensed things very strongly from a young age, and I remember sensing something wasn't right with my mom and dad. Mom was crying way too much, and although she always prayed, her prayers seemed a little bit more like cries to Jesus. I remember how beautiful I have always thought my mom was, but these days her eyes held sadness. I had the feeling of a sick pit in my stomach as I would notice my dad not acting the way he always had before. I knew Mom and Dad were arguing, and I don't like the way the house felt. The oak tree was still standing, but something from the roots of our family seemed to be shaking.

I wasn't wrong, our foundation was shaking and our lives as a family of five would no longer be. I was soon to be the child of "divorced parents". I remember when I would hear of people getting divorces as a child, I thought that only happened to "bad people," people in jail, or people who were poor, not people who lived in a suburb, or people just not quite like what seemed to be the perfect family, and a pastor's family, that's not heard of. But now I was a part of that club, and ever since that period in my life, I realize painful things happen to everyone. No one is immune. I just wish we didn't have to learn that so young.

It seemed to happen quickly, my parents were getting a divorce, and we had to leave the church, we had to turn in the car that the church paid for, everything that seemed to bring security to our home was gone, including my dad, the one who I looked at as my protector, provider, and now I felt uncovered.

My brother, the oldest, was immediately handed the baton of grow up quick and be the man. This wasn't done intentionally to him at all, but he felt it in his heart, and at the same time, his heart was broken. He was too young to carry this responsibility and weight. We all became what we had to be at that moment, and we became a different kind of family. Not the family I had dreamed we would be—no pictures of family picnics, no beach pictures with Dad in the center holding my baby sister. The picture changed, and now we have to readjust everything in our lives. It didn't seem fair; I liked it the way it was. I remember feeling ashamed in a way and embarrassed, almost guilty as if it was my fault.

Did it change the heart of my mom towards God? No, as a matter of fact, I felt Jesus more than ever in her; I saw Him in her tears, in her joy, in her actions and lifestyle, and there began my testimony, for little did I know that I would one-day face pain way greater than what I was facing now. I watched my mom grow through her pain, trust God continually, and it showed me so much about faith. I was blessed even at that time, for I had the greatest example of how to handle it. My mom stood strong for us; even though weak in body and mind, her faith didn't waver.

I want to say thank you to my mom and dad because my parents never made me feel uncomfortable. I loved them both, and they made a friendship work enough, and I am sure at times it wasn't easy, but they did it for their kids. I remember them both being at graduations,

RHONDA LUCAS

birthdays, or get-togethers, and they would talk and be civil, grown-up adults to one another. Another testimony was forgiveness. It's easy to say you can do it, but until required to live it out, it's a different story.

We grew together as a family of four, we hurt at times, we lost at times, we struggled financially a lot at times, but we made it. I loved High School and was blessed with some amazing, incredible friends that I am still friends with today. These friends were the kind you could go over and get in their closet, swap clothes, come sleepover after a date, laugh until your stomach hurts. I remember a lot of things, but I don't remember stressing too much about life. A Dr. Pepper and barbecue chips and time with my friends, and I was happy. I was on the Drill Team, and oh, the memories we made on that bus en route to games. Homecoming was such fun and all the things that go with being involved in school. I hear so many times now about young people dreading school, anxiety over the exams, and peer pressure. I know I had it to some extent, but nothing like these young people face now.

Well, soon I was graduating from Stockbridge High School, the Class of 1985. I really didn't have a clue what I wanted to do. Back then, you started school younger, and I graduated at the age of 17, and maybe now looking back, I feel that's really young and maybe a little too young to be thrown out into the world of careers. Being in a single-family home with one small income didn't allow me to be picky about college.

After graduation, I worked for a friend in his accounting department at a mortgage company and learned more than I did in those college courses I took. I was learning life skills, how to go to lunch with a bunch of people and pretend you know what they are talking about, how to drive to work when you feel sick in traffic, how to answer the phones with a smile in your voice, how to do accounting on a ledger. So many mistakes I made and so much I learned. I was learning to be a grown-up, and sometimes it wasn't too fun. I learned easily that the paycheck doesn't go too far when you spend it the first day you get paid; that outfit to wear on my date wasn't really worth it. Oh, the things we learn and sometimes have to learn on our own.

It was a year after graduation, and we were dead into the long hot summers of Georgia. You see, it wasn't easy to find a pool. We didn't live in a neighborhood with swim and tennis; most of them at that time didn't have amenities like that. We didn't have cell phones to call a friend and ask if we could come use their pool. We would almost pray that someone would get a burden to invite us over so we could share in their wealth of a pool. It was a hot summer, and when weekends approached, I just wanted to layout and swim. So many times, I remember my mom finally driving us to a pool that was at least thirty minutes away and the car breaking down. Again, no cell phone; we had to walk to a home, knock on their door, and pray they would let us in to use their phone.

Gosh, we have it so much easier as far as communication. That's why I am not one to make a big stink about a young person at a pool that isn't a member. If they aren't hurting anything or anyone, just let them swim. A lot of my compassion comes from being in the place that someone is or has been through. I will never not give credit to our little town that had a man-made lake, "Swan Lake. I don't even want to know what that round man-made, circle of water consisted of. All I know is I made lots of memories there and never got sick, call it God's grace, and maybe a little bit too much sun.

That summer seemed just a summer of playing it as I went. I knew I wasn't in the greatest place of my walk with God and didn't know what I should do, wanted to do, and where I should be. Yet, as I reflect on that summer of 1986, I know it was the time that I learned for me that it is easier to be obedient, and that is where I begin to walk in the beginning of my story. It was just the beginning of my story, but mine isn't the fairytale one, no castles or big tiaras to be placed upon my head, yet I found my prince.

I wasn't even willing to go to church that Sunday morning in late August, almost 19 in one month, and my mom was still making me go to church, sometimes I could wiggle my way out of it, but I just knew today wasn't the day. Have you ever, as a teenager, just gave in because maybe the night before you stayed up too late and even you didn't want to argue with your parents? Or maybe feeling a little guilt over knowing the lifestyle wasn't the ideal. Well, that was me. If you are looking for a book about a perfect girl, this isn't the one. I wasn't wild, but I sure wasn't perfect.

As moms, we all have facial expressions and movements we make to our child to let them know that we aren't playing. I knew that when my mom would tilt her head to the side and say, "Rhonda, I meant what I said," I knew it wasn't a day to play. I remember I felt anger towards her for being treated like a child, I was almost 19, and this just didn't sit well with me. But on that morning, I couldn't come up with an excuse; my throat didn't hurt, I didn't have plans, and she didn't care anyway. I was going to church, and my mom had now changed into a military mom, and I was in combat training.

I remember the long car drive to church; you see, we didn't have cell phones to hide our anger and bury our faces in; we didn't have social media to give us another conversation to talk about. The radio may or may not have been working that morning, and no Bluetooth or "Air Pods" to give the atmosphere a change. Yup, just dead silence and a daughter mad at her mom because she made me go to church.

It was all kind of strange when looking back, and with all the changes in the world and women's movements, we would now have a complaint against the young guy you will now hear about. Life was different then, and I kind of miss the innocence. Here we are at this massive church and seated on the front row this Sunday to fill in any empty seats. You see, we were seated further back because I did let my mom know that I would not be sitting up front. Again, I didn't win; they spotted her and signaled for us to move right up front. This was where staff sat… Yup, they sat right up front and CLOSE. I was annoyed, and I didn't care how good the worship was today. I wasn't about to show one emotion except for anger, and then… I felt myself get even angrier as I felt every move that I made being recorded. This church we attended was full of people, and cameras were large, and there were several of them on platforms elevated from the normal seating.

I for sure thought this was a setup, and my angry face was being made fun of by all the camera crew. This crazy guy wouldn't take the camera off of me; no I didn't take it as a compliment. I took it as I must have something in my nose (yes, going back to my runny nose on the bus), or something just is off with me. The more I felt the camera on me, the madder I became. I don't remember anything that the message was about that day. I was just aggravated and yet curious about this guy. Yes, I looked back to see who this person was that the pastor had to stop during his message and say, "Matt, please put the camera on me." *Who the heck is Matt, and what does he want from me? What did I do to deserve to be humiliated? Did he know I wasn't living my best life? Did God tell him to get me saved?*

I had to discuss this with my mom on the car ride home. I remember saying, "Mom, whomever that was who was running the camera was so annoying, I will never sit up that close again." I still, to this day, remember my mom and the face she made when I said that; she smiled so big and confidently said, "Oh, that's Matt, isn't he handsome?" She continued to smile as she drove; I continued to be upset as my day was not as I had planned. My response was so typical, "No, he's annoying," yet under the attitude, I was thinking, *Yes, he was annoying but handsome.* Young people, please read this over and over, sometimes moms know best, even when they don't even know themselves why they are so determined for you to go to church that particular day; just trust them.

It didn't take him too long to call, it was Labor Day, and I was home in my room when my mom brought the phone up to me and said, "Matt is on the phone." She forgot to share the night before she had given him my number at church. Thank God she didn't make me go back that night to the service. I feel in her heart she was very pleased with what transpired that morning and would just relish in it.

The courtship began slowly after some persuading from Matt, Mom, and even some of my mom's friends. When I say slowly, I mean, I wasn't playing easy to get with this guy. I think I was afraid at the time of what it would require of me. I grew up in church and now can finally get some space. Does this mean I have to be at church all the time? I am not so sure about attending every Sunday and everything in between.

I grew up where we would spend all day at church, and so often, the pews became my bed; I don't long for this anymore. I kind of like being able to stay at my friends on a Saturday night and not feel pressured to be at church the next day.

So many things had transpired in my life in regard to church; I had seen my parents get hurt and go through so much. Why? Because church isn't perfect, as long as there are people, there will be issues. I wasn't quite ready again to do the whole "church scene" and lifestyle. But you see, slowly I began to fall in love not just with the handsome, charismatic Matt, but the man I saw he already was and would become even more; I fell in love with his love for Jesus. No, he wasn't perfect, and you can already tell I sure wasn't. But once I fell, I fell hard and knew I wanted to spend the rest of my life with him.

There are so many details in between the years of dating and our wedding day, lots of laughter, growing pains, learning, and finding out how to stretch a penny, yup a penny. You see, the Mercedes car he picked me up in several times wasn't his, many times his car didn't work, or someone was borrowing it, the money we both had spending on ourselves didn't seem to quite be enough to combine for marriage and full responsibilities. How in the world would we be able to get married and live in an apartment when just getting Little Caesar's pizza was a challenge? But we made it and had great dates. Our favorite was when we went to the popular Friday's restaurant on a Friday. You have to be old enough to appreciate the days when Friday's restaurant was the couple's hot spot to eat for a date, and an order of potato skins full of everything was a must, then the hot brownie with vanilla ice cream. Wow, it takes me back to so many memories, and I wouldn't trade one of them.

He won't mind if I share, but the true test came when he lost his license for a year because all of his speeding tickets from traveling, even in Hawaii, caught up with him. Yup, many days and nights, he would ride his bike to see me, and it wasn't a short bike ride. I did a lot of driving and picking him up, and I was not angry but anticipating seeing his face. That was love and work. Now we call an Uber to pick up our date when we can't drive. We really, in so many ways, have become the generation of "fix it, and now". It was worth it all, and at the time, that seemed so hard and frustrating, but that was just the beginning of what would be required of us.

We had dated a while now, and it was time for more. We were tired of saying goodnight to each other, and we both knew we weren't the type to wait until life is perfect; let's make it perfect together. I didn't make the list of pros and cons and personality tests. They didn't have an enneagram test back then. I didn't know if I was a 10, 2, 4, or a, b, c, and d. I think I was a little bit of all of it, HA! We didn't ask each other if we had 401K or what the monthly balance of our checking accounts was. We hadn't heard of Dave Ramsey and his financial advice, so we just prayed the checks we wrote wouldn't bounce before we had to go physically to deposit our paycheck. Yes, again, there was no phone application to take a picture of our deposits. You had to open the mailbox and get the slip from the bank that was like a neon poster "your check was returned". That was always a nice feeling; if you didn't get the check in by 2:00 p.m. at the bank, you could expect that in the mail in a few days.

I just knew I loved Matt, this handsome 6'4", kind, compassionate man, my superman, and I wanted to spend the rest of my life doing this thing called "life" with him. I didn't see the future of what we would face together, and that's actually what makes life so beautiful. I won't go into the long details, and the ups and downs all the ins and outs of the premarital journey, but on October 14, 1989, Matt and I made a vow before God, family, and friends to love one another, in sickness and in health, for richer and for poorer, in joy and in SORROW, in joy and in SORROW, SORROW, SORROW…

Hold on, this isn't a book of sorrow and woe is me; I don't get stuck in my pain, but just as I write, the words resonate in my head. We say those vows at times with such innocence and confidence and almost a ritual, and many times we don't stop to think that it could actually be my life with him. That day, I didn't even realize what I was repeating as I looked in my husband's eyes; I just knew it was part of the ceremony, and I just wanted to be his wife and give him a kiss and run out the door. SORROW wasn't the word I was paying attention to; it was, "You may now kiss your bride." Maybe I was naive, stupid, and too innocent, but on that day, I never ever thought of one bad thing, one sad thing, but just that I was getting married, and I get to build a life with this guy.

I have found Matt, and I always have a little story behind the "perfect" and no flaws at the wedding, we just wanted to drive off like they do in the movies with our driver Roger, (Matt's brother) and look rich and all together, but of course the car wouldn't start. And let's be honest married people, we wanted to get to the hotel, no time for broken down cars. It would have been really embarrassing if we had it on what we now have called Instagram live. We were trying to look all together and can't even get the darn car to start.

I wanted to get to the hotel and start to enjoy this life together. We just didn't seem to have too much good luck with cars, so many issues between licenses and cars broken into (another story that happened right before our wedding). We did laugh, and that's so much of who we are, and it started at the beginning, it was a laugh or cry from pretty much very early on, and we began to laugh at our inconveniences and things that were just par for the course. It seemed way easier on the heart.

The vows we said on that day mean so much more now. As I write this, the words "Till death do us part" it echoes and screams loudly in my mind. Why yes, of course, that's normal; it is part of the tradition of wedding vows that were spoken many, many years ago. They were vows we could recite just by watching movies and attending other's weddings. We will age, become grandparents, great grandparents, maybe retire by the beach, we will die as our bodies one day give out, but it will be years and years before we face the word "death". I honor those vows more now than I did that day. I couldn't possibly really know what those words meant until actually having to live them out. We had moments where the "poorer" seemed all too real, but not to the extent I see others suffering. No, we couldn't afford a house right away, very often we had to pray our cars would make it home. We know what it is to look at the gas gauge and pray it doesn't move much till payday. Yet, even that wasn't that bad.

Sickness and health, we had some sick days in the beginning, but I mean a cold or stomach bug, not dealing at that point with cancer in my family that resulted in loss. So, these vows were beautiful and said with a heart of purity, but they weren't real to us yet. You see, the test hadn't knocked on the doors of our hearts yet, and that's something God doesn't show you in advance. It is something He provides grace when needed. Life isn't like the puzzle already put together. When we purchase a boxed puzzle, we can see what the outcome is going to look like. All those tiny pieces that are blank or shadowed with just a little color, the corner pieces that we want to find first to get the frame done, all have an end result that we can see.

Yet, God doesn't allow us to see how the picture of our life ends up. Why? Because only He knows the outcome, the blank pieces, the dark pieces that will create a beautiful landscape when put with the pieces of a bright sky. He doesn't want us to live in fear of our outcome. He often holds back those big pieces that make the puzzle come together so that we can be molded into His image, so we can learn to trust. He makes the beautiful places; He makes the edges smooth; His canvas is the perfect puzzle.

I Just Want to Be a Mom

I often question myself, why haven't I ever been a huge dreamer? Of course, I have dreams and goals, but I mean the kind to be in the Olympics or get every degree, earn millions. Why haven't I thought of dreams so big they were so out of my reach? It wasn't that I didn't have visions of better, but I had a stirring and longing in my heart to love something more than myself, more than my dream, and that was to be a mom. I dabbed in the thought of becoming a lawyer; I wanted to fight for what was right and the law. I hated anything of injustice and would argue with anyone if I felt something was wrong. I just didn't think it would anyway be possible for me to become a lawyer, and now I realize it would have been possible, and I would have been good at arguing and defending someone. At that time, I knew nothing of scholarships, and I didn't have anyone to pay for my school and probably didn't honestly have the confidence and discipline at that time to pursue it. I did, however, have a desire burning within me of something I knew that I could do.

I was the young bride who couldn't wait for the words "Let's try to have children." I couldn't wait until we could financially afford to buy a box of diapers. I worked downtown for a well-known insurance company, and I had a lot of friendships with my coworkers, and my job was good, but after a few years, I wanted more. While working, I learned discipline and getting up early, putting on a game face, and sitting in traffic for hours. Yes, even then, Atlanta traffic was bad. I remember crying on the way home from work, missing Matt, and wanting to have an extension of him with me 24/7. The urge and that longing for that little boy or girl were becoming so deep, so real. I know we can have both a career and be a mom, I admire those with great businesses all the while being a mom, but for me, at that time, I just wanted them all to myself. I envisioned a little Matt running around, just saying "Mommy," cozy nights at home, baseball games, birthday parties, Christmas with Santa, yup maybe not too big of a goal, it wouldn't be written in the bright lights anywhere "Rhonda CEO of her home, inventor of being a mom". No, it was just the title so many already have, and it may seem so small, but this would be my "Oscar," my medal of honor; I wanted to be good at this thing called motherhood. It was my prayer to have the gift of life formed in me and brought into this earth and to raise up a child; that was what I wanted. Yes, it was enough, a gift of more than enough.

It didn't come easy while trying. I had two miscarriages and one that required surgery. I anxiously knew what it was to take the pregnancy test, and it be negative. Nothing compared to what other women go through trying to conceive; I was thankful for a doctor that realized this could probably be easily fixed, so the diagnosis came that I needed more estrogen to carry my baby to full term, and it was finally corrected. The day we saw the sonogram and found out I was carrying a boy, we were elated, we were blessed, and Matt was having a son. It wasn't always sunshine because I admit I began to allow fear to creep in because of the miscarriages I had. I was afraid every time I didn't feel the baby move or something didn't feel right. Fear creeps in so easily, and in some ways, it was normal to be this way. The protective mom instinct was already in full swing. Looking back, I wish I would have fought that fear more with the word of God; I wish I wouldn't have given in so easily to those thoughts. I didn't care, boy or girl, I would be grateful. When we found out the sex of our baby, I was elated and ready to shop for all things baby blue. I knew at that moment that this boy was going to do great and mighty things even before he was born.

I carried him in my stomach with such great pride. I shopped for the cutest baby clothes, he was my prince, and he would wear knee socks and the white lace-up Stride Rite shoes; he was royalty to me. I waited, prayed, cried, and sought God for this child, and soon oh so soon, he would capture our hearts.

I worked for a great company at the time, had coworkers that became friends. The drive to work was long, but those drives were my time to think and get my attitude straight in traffic before facing the day. The drive became longer as the pregnancy neared the end. I remember thinking I can't do this much longer, Caleb must have been thinking the same thing. Then full of surprises, Caleb Matthew came three weeks early the day of my shower. My first baby shower, I was excited. I was going to get lots of presents, the adorable tiny soft baby clothes and blankets, hopefully, the stroller we needed, the bassinet, and we would eat good cake and take pictures with family and friends. Now, remember back then, we couldn't immediately look at them like we can now. It was a process, and I had never heard of the word selfie at that time.

My mom was hosting the shower; the house was perfect with soft touches of powder blue here and there, flowers on tables, everything was "shower ready" for the following day. Do any of you women get a little "crazy" before hosting an event at your house or having company over? My husband thinks I become a little over the top as I need everything scrubbed and perfect, and I think I learned it from my mom because she was in crazy mode. We innately feel that people will notice if our drawers aren't clean and the blinds have a touch of dust on them. It's a great way to get things done around the house; just plan an event.

But God's timing isn't always ours, is it? Moms, I know you can relate to this, and probably many of you have gone through this. We leak, ok, we leak, and then you are so far along in your pregnancy you just maybe feel you dripped a little urine; well, mine was not a little drip but almost like a vase of water flowing down my legs as I slept. I really did think that I had wet the bed. Now it's just the change of life and hot flashes that take me back to that day. But I awoke to tell my mom, and she didn't look too pleased; this wasn't anything she had prepared to happen on this special day. This was the day she wanted to experience, and she had worked hard for; she was celebrating her first grandchild. She so softly spoke and said, "Honey, this is nothing more than a little drip until she saw this wasn't a drip but a consistent flow of water. She still was praying the prayer of faith because, after all, she did introduce me to the father of our baby, so the least I could do is honor her by not going into labor.

So, you understand my water broke; not only was it the day of my shower, but Matt was in Tampa, Florida, at the time for training for his job. There are things in life we have no control over, and this was one of them. Caleb was coming into this world, and he was ready to make his entrance. This was not going by my birthing plan whatsoever. Flights had to be changed for Matt, and I was admitted to the hospital and the doctor's words, "Well Rhonda, you are going to have a baby."

Fifteen hours later, as much as Caleb wanted to come into this world, it wasn't coming easy. I now feel a part of him was comforted in the safety of my womb, he was probably listening to the confusion already out there in the world, and it felt safe inside; there was trust there. He couldn't decide and still tossing and turning in my womb, he was taken by c-section, and that day January 16, 1993, my real life began. Yes, at the age of 26, I realized it was no longer about me; I am no longer able to put myself first all the time, I no longer am worried about my needs, but this was the day I truly learned how to love unselfishly. I stared at this beautiful creation that was swaddled in a blanket and placed in my arms, our moment, this was our time, this little bundle was completely dependent on me, and it was my job to take care of him. I felt such honor; I felt that God really trusted and loved me. How was I so blessed to get to do this amazing job?

We all know at that moment there is a love so completely unexpected that comes out of us; there is a depth of love we had only heard about. Whether you have birthed your child or adopted, there is a love that cannot be explained in words—A magical love. Something changes in the heart the minute you hold your baby; your heart begins to beat differently, now stronger and faster, I feel because it's now beating for two. You are so full of overwhelming admiration for this little creature God has entrusted us with. At that moment, we already wonder how we ever lived without them, don't we?

I felt there was never life before having Caleb; I mean a life that was fulfilled the way I had dreamed of. January 16, 1993, changed

RHONDA LUCAS

me forever. I am glad I only saw him as a baby at that moment; I am glad God only gave me the strength for that moment because my heart would never ever been able to grasp that one day my trust in the creator of Caleb would be questioned.

Before I formed you in the womb, I knew you, before you were born, I set you apart....

—Jeremiah 1:5 NIV

No One Told Me There Would Be Days Like

As you read this book, I pray you feel and sense my honesty in every line. I have never, ever been good at lying. I find it easier to be flawed than to try to be perfect. The reason for that is, you will find my attempt at being perfect doesn't last long. Even for surprises, I just can't lie.

Caleb was an easy baby; he wasn't fussy; he was happy unless hungry. He made me feel I can do this many, many times over without fail. I was made for babies; I need to have more. I must be the best mom; my son is so easy; I am doing this all right. I was the Dr. Laura of moms, but what the heck was I thinking?

Now, I had a few fear issues myself. I mean, if he even felt one little, tiny degree warm, he was at the doctor; if his cheeks weren't that rosy color he always had, we were at the doctor's door. I was that over conscious mom, the first-time mom, where possibly I still had too much time on my hands, maybe? Exhaustion hadn't even really hit me when Caleb was born, I know I had moments or days, but I was so thrilled and proud of this child of mine. I didn't care if I missed sleep; I didn't want to miss a moment with this angel. As months went by, his chubby round face grew even cuter, the blonde hair came in so beautifully, time was flying by, and his little spirit of joy had already evolved. Do you moms ever feel that way? There is a newness of life that we feel with the first child. By the second child, we have loosened up a bit, and by the third child, we are way more relaxed and realize a little dirt won't hurt them, and neither will drinking from a hose once in a while. I still go back to the days where we lived off the hose water; we didn't come in for a Dasani when playing outside, we played till the streetlights went on and drank from the hose, and we made it; that's another book in itself.

Caleb was seriously the baby and toddler that would capture attention; he would light up a room. He loved people; he didn't really go through the phase of being afraid of others. Caleb, from a young age, made everyone feel loved, he was sensitive when something wasn't right, and he was truly a mommy and daddy's boy. I would say he carried with him a contagious personality, one that made people want to be closer to him.

I already felt he was growing so fast, and the next phase possibly was soon around the corner, or should I say growing rounder in my belly?

"You are having a girl," the words sounded too perfect. I have a boy, and now I am blessed to have a girl? This can't be my life; this is the ideal life, the life I dreamed of. I would love to tell myself a lie and say I was the adorable pregnant woman with just all belly. Oh, I had the belly and maybe the entire body of a donut. Not my greatest confidence moments, but I was happy.

I felt so blessed; I am able to stay home with my son and now expecting a baby girl. Life was beautiful; I mean beautiful. And beautiful she was; Sharon Mackenzie born on 9–3–1995, two and a half years after Caleb was born; she had a head full of dark hair and chubby cheeks. I was so happy to have a healthy baby that immediately took to breastfeeding and already seemed to be starving for food and my attention.

Before we left the hospital, she had a severe case of jaundice, and I could sense a lot of worry in me beginning to appear; and I allowed it again, and I realized I should not have taken every negative thought to heart and let it take hold of my mind. I wish I could go back and shake myself. She had her own little tanning bed the hospital set up at our home, little glasses, and all. I wasn't able to hold her much for about a week, only to feed and change her because of her blood count. Her color had to change to that rosy healthy look, and numbers had to be normal before she could sleep in her bassinet. Yes, that perfect, girly beautiful bassinet that I had ready for months wasn't even touched. The room was all perfect and ready, but was I?

I am writing this, so you will know where I am coming from. A little bit of what has brought me to this point that I was at is the ugly word "perfection". I think all too often we want to pretend we have it all together; we want to share how good we are doing at this job called motherhood. We don't want to share our fears and failures because we are afraid of feeling weak next to the other moms. Motherhood is a learning experience, and for some of us, we may feel overwhelmed. All of a sudden, someone is completely dependent on us, and we don't feel good enough, and we begin to question ourselves, and the strength we had so much of at the beginning is not there… what happened to me? But now, looking back, this was all preparation. What prepared me for my earthquake? We all have a history, and this is mine, but I bet you may just find a little bit of your story in one or more of these paragraphs.

So, we named her Sharon Mackenzie, and she's now 23 as I write this, but she wasn't an easy baby. She was a true breastfed baby who wanted her mom 24/7. At first, it's an honor; she loves me and only me; I am the only one who can provide her nourishment, then it becomes life draining. Mackenzie didn't want her dad, her grandma, or anyone; she only wanted me, and I needed help. I needed a break away, time to take a bath alone without her crying because she could sense I wasn't right next to her. I would become very brave at times and leave her with family, and numerous times, I would have to go home and console the family member who watched her and try to pay them a large sum of money for the pain they suffered from listening to her scream. I didn't have videos, vlogs, podcasts, and anything to listen to, and at that point, I don't think I could even hear any more noise.

Meanwhile, I was keeping the perfect house. I would not go to bed without the house being spotless, no matter how late it was or how little sleep I had. Now, this wasn't a fancy home, just a three-bedroom ranch with a basement. And yet it was our home, and I was going to have it clean and cozy. I was the mom who wouldn't let them leave the house in play clothes; their hair had to be perfect. I was the annoying mom, who annoyed myself more than anyone. I was constantly cleaning their hands in fear of germs; some virus that came from God knows that it wasn't entering my home. I seriously could feel myself getting on my own nerves. Do you all ever feel that way? I will be so annoyed, and it's just because I am annoying myself. I look around, and no one is even near me to get on my nerves; it's just me.

On top of wanting the perfect children, house, and lifestyle, I thought I also needed to try my best to look perfect. I got on this exercise kick and diet, where I was determined to be thinner than ever and all while she was draining every bit of calories out of me. Let me stress this, I am all for exercising and a healthy lifestyle, but when it begins to dominate your mind and control how you feel about yourself if you miss a day, then something may be off. Now, this may throw all of you for a loop; you may even think I am a writer for a comedy book, but I was down to a size two. My kids were looking good and healthy, house clean, and mom slowly falling apart, I mean, falling apart, my legs felt like Jell-O, and every bit of strength was gone. My body aches were becoming too common, and yet it all looked so good from the outside, but inside I knew it wasn't good at all. I was weak on the inside and outside, and I felt myself dying.

Mackenzie was almost a year and walking and no longer breast-feeding, she was becoming so much easier, and the attachment had lessened. Caleb and Mackenzie were already the best of buddies and began to entertain each other. They were together non-stop, and although younger, she was the boss. Only now she was happy, and all of a sudden, I wasn't. I remember certain things as if it were yesterday, and one of those times was the day that I found myself obsessing over the windows. I kept going back every time I would see one spot and spray Windex on it, cleaning, cleaning, and cleaning. It felt it was something I could have control over, I couldn't control my feelings of anxiety creeping up, but I could keep cleaning this window.

My spirit was empty, and my soul wasn't fed with anything of substance. This is what I wanted, to be a mom, a stay at home mom, the perfect house, the perfect marriage and children, and yet all I wanted to do was sit and stare. I began to feel guilty on top of everything else

I was feeling, and we all know guilt is truly a sickening feeling. I felt guilty for not being happy, guilty for having this beautiful life and struggling to get up. It made it worse because I should feel like the happiest girl in the world, and yet I am dying inside. Let me say this, we should never judge someone just because they do seem to have the "good life," it doesn't mean they aren't facing battles. At this point, I felt no one would understand, and I would be the one being judged.

This part of this book is actually a part of the first book I never got published but was edited and never made the next step. So, why not combine a portion of my book that sits with dust on the papers but yet has even more meaning now.

The book I wrote was called Who Hit the Light Switch. Why that title? Well, about nine months after she was born, I continued to lose weight, my mind was foggy, and I had racing thoughts. I continued to do everything as I normally would, but it didn't come without lots of tears and lots of pushing. I remember this one morning while preparing to sing with my mom and sister that evening for a big event in town; I found myself barely able to walk. I thought I had the flu, some type of infection, and something wasn't right, but tomorrow will be different, yes, tomorrow. My arms and legs felt like rubber bands, and this wasn't me; I rarely get sick. I remember not being able to concentrate that evening as we sang in front of a large crowd; I just wanted to get home; home will make me feel better. I just want to get through these songs and run and escape from the noise. Tomorrow will be better...

But tomorrow wasn't different, nor the next day, or weeks, and even months had gone by. Finally, I gave in and went to a doctor who told me I was "too thin" and felt I was suffering from Post-Partum Depression. I looked at the doctor as if he was crazy, "No, that isn't me, not my life." I have a good life; that's for those with sad stories, those that have bigger issues, abuse, poverty, those people have a reason to be depressed, not me. My life is happy; I have a relationship with Jesus; my heart is full of good things. I will never forget that day as long as I live, as the doctor, with his scribbling handwriting, wrote out a prescription for an antidepressant, and the prescription was torn up as I left. This will not be my journey. This isn't the puzzle I purchased where all the pieces were full of color and perfectly put together, I don't like this picture of me, and I won't have this label attached to me. Post-Partum? No thanks, doctor, not me.

I remember going home, and I wept as I told my mom; I struggled to take a bite of anything and could barely pick up my babies. From morning till night, I would play worship songs, and back then, there wasn't nearly a selection like we have now, but whatever I could listen to, I did. I continuously put on TBN, TD Jakes was always on at the right time and the right word to give me enough strength to hang on for another moment. All the while, Caleb and Mackenzie drew closer and closer together as I fell apart. Never for a moment would I allow myself to rest; if I would rest, it was a sign of weakness and giving in to this awful title "postpartum depression". It began to haunt me, I began to have nightmares, and suddenly everything about depression was on the television. I couldn't escape this; no matter how many scriptures I quoted, songs I sang, prayers I prayed, nothing was changing, except me.

I will never forget the morning my mom had spent the night because the night before Matt and I had an event for the youth group of our church. I thought if I just continue to give out, God will surely honor it, and I will feel happy tomorrow. I will be better; the more I do, the sooner my recovery. I didn't for a moment doubt that God could heal me in an instant. Now I know why it didn't happen that way; I see the bigger piece of the puzzle because even then, I was being taught that I cannot do this in my own strength. I have to be completely and totally dependent on Him. This particular morning was the morning I realized my healing wasn't coming the way I had hoped. It didn't come through the natural doctors I had tried (yet they are awesome and because I had waited until it had gotten so bad they couldn't help). It didn't come from traveling to women's conferences out of state for my healing. It didn't come from going to every prayer meeting I could and being prayed over. No, it didn't come that way, and now I know why. I had a little thing called "PRIDE". And yet this morning,

I had no pride left. I remember barely able to walk into Caleb's room where my mom was lying in Caleb's twin bed, in my pajamas with tears falling down my cheeks, I went to my mom and said, "Mom, if I don't get help, I am going to die." I still feel those words coming out of my mouth as if it were yesterday, although so painful, this was the day that I began to heal. I don't know how, but the very moment I spoke, I need help, I felt healing coming.

I was taken back to a place in my mind and heart of where I had judged anyone who had to get on any medicine of any type; I was taken back to the place where I may have labeled someone in my mind because they were depressed. Now I was that person, and I was being placed at the altar to be healed, to have all my misconceptions wiped away and swallow my pride. Pride is one of the ugliest things that comes so easily. It comes when we think what we accomplish, do, or succeed in, is from our own strength. It's ugly and destructive.

I was broken and weak, and I knew what I had to do. I called my OB/GYN and asked for the mildest lowest anti-depressant they had, and after much prayer and research, I began to heal. I took the prescription prescribed to me and knew it wouldn't be an overnight miracle, but I was sure willing to try. I know it's hard to believe, (Laughter is inserted you just can't hear it.), but I gained weight back, I found the sun was actually really shining, I found joy in shopping again, I found hope in life, and I felt the guilt of being sad leaving me as I fell even more in love with my family.

Can I be honest with you and you be honest with yourself? I want to suggest something if you are going through anything like this, stop and listen. Take care of yourself; it's ok not to feel right and seek answers for it. Please, my friends, don't be afraid to seek help and don't be afraid to share with others, don't allow yourself to think it won't get better and for thoughts of negative destruction to happen. There is treatment, and God is able to heal and also to bring those to you to help you. I don't want anyone to feel they are alone and isolated. I want you to know there is light beyond your temporary place of darkness.

I want to share (below) a little bit of the book that I wrote a book before and never had it published, but I feel to share some of it with you. Maybe you need it.

> This place of depression in 1996 brought me to my knees literally. I realized everything I thought I was, had nothing to do with His plan for me; it was my plan. I found that deep inside of me, I held a lot of pride, and this experience knocked it out of me.
>
> —Who Hit the Light Switch

I wrote that book because I wanted to share my story with other women, so they could know they aren't alone, and no, you aren't crazy, and yes, you are a good mom, and Rhonda made it, and so will you. I wish I would have had the book published, but as I read back on the chapters, it's hard to comprehend what has transpired since I wrote that book. Wow, so grateful God doesn't allow us to see our future. He protects us in ways we can't imagine. It could be an epic sequel *Who Hit the Light Switch* and then to *Just Once*. No, you can't make this stuff up.

Whatever I write, I pray speaks to some part of you and brings hope. If there is any advice I would give to you, let me tell you this; it's only because I have walked this valley. During this season of my life, I would wake up every morning with hope even when the day was still dark.

I would shower, put makeup on, and get dressed. When battling anxiety and depression, we have to be careful not to allow our days to feel exactly like our nights. I know the emotions can feel dark even during the day, but we have to mentally and physically separate them. It's morning, and it's the beginning of a new day; awaken with hope, and when you are getting out of your bed, pat yourself on the back and say, "By the Grace of Almighty God, I will get through this."

I can promise you that you will get through this. Since I first experienced it years back, there has been so much more research, and healthy options are even more available than it was ten years ago. I remember one thing I would always speak to myself, "Today, I will feel better, no matter what I think, I will feel better." Speak words over yourself and speak them out loud; you probably won't feel it or believe it at first, and even if you still don't, then keep going. Who cares, what could go wrong, you will feel crazy? Grace abounds in our darkest moments and hours. It abounds when life makes no sense when things arise in our bodies and minds that shouldn't be there. He is aware; get used to me writing that. HE IS AWARE.

This wasn't an overnight healing, oh how I would love to say it was; I would love to tell you it will go away quickly. It was a process of faith, daily, minute by minute, it was a process of letting go of things that I thought I could control, it was often many times telling myself, "This too shall pass." I wish it could have been really fast, but it wasn't; that would have been too easy.

I thought dark days couldn't be any darker, but God was preparing me for what would lie ahead.

I can do all things through Christ Who Strengthens me.

—Philippians 4:13 NKJV

Just Trying to Keep Up With the Jones, and I Can't Keep Up

Shortly after becoming a mom, I realized the competition was fierce. The competition to have the smartest child, the one who could walk first, read first, the most athletic, who was attending the best school. All of this was a pressure I was already feeling; oh my gosh, I want to slap the old me. I hated the labels we already put on our child and the expectations we put on ourselves to make them become something; it can be overwhelming.

I felt myself giving in to what I thought was expected of me, and it was tough because I just wanted to enjoy them, and yet I felt if I didn't keep up, my child wouldn't be in the best schools, the best classes, etc. and sometimes they weren't, and we began to be ok with that. I gave up a lot of the comparison thing with my children after the third grade. It was mentally exhausting.

I began to realize my enough may not be someone else's, and I was good with that. And I began to learn, yes, learn, slowly and surely. Whatever stage they were in would be ok, even if it meant I wasn't. That was easier back then, social media hadn't even begun, and yet the human nature in us was still trying to keep up. I pray for parents, women and men, and yes, we can gain wisdom from others, and we should have others to share concerns and things we are going through or celebrating, but not compete with; there is enough of that we will have to face throughout life.

I knew we weren't done with having children; shoot I would have loved to have had five, but I truly believe God gives you what you need because He is the only one who sees the bigger picture. It was three years after Mackenzie was born that I was given my baby boy Micah Seth a beautiful, healthy baby boy, and we felt complete. I will tell you a funny little story, he was conceived at Disney World; maybe it was all the magic we felt and happiness. Just a suggestion, but if you are thinking about having another child go to Disney World. We soon were now the Party-of-Five, and we loved this new title; it all felt right, and we were just happy.

Everything began just to work out, and life was seriously going well. I had my health under control again, I had no postpartum with Micah, and I couldn't thank God enough. I took nothing for granted. Did anxiety try to rear its head up? Of course, but once you learn the triggers and how to fight it, then you know when it's starting to come back on, and that's when I check myself. Am I doing too much? Am I spending time with God? Am I focusing too much on everyone else's needs? If you are one who suffers from this, be aware of what triggers it. Sometimes it could be a lack of sleep, too much caffeine, and possibly our diet? More times than not, it can be just plain life and that thing we have called HORMONES. We have to learn to fight back and speak to yourself,

> Be Anxious for nothing, but in everything by prayer and supplication, with thanksgiving, let your requests be made known to God.
>
> —Philippians 4:6–7 NKJV

ALSO, when I do have those days, I don't freak out anymore. I just know it's a day, and this too shall pass, and if it doesn't for you, then please seek help. We aren't meant to carry these burdens alone. Our mental health matters; we cannot dismiss it, ignore it; it's real and serious. There is hope, though, and there are healing and answers to so many of the things we don't think we can get help for. I guarantee you someone you know is going through it also, share with them and allow others to know what you are battling. As women, we can see it as a weakness and keep it to ourselves, which only makes it worse. We hold in guilt that shouldn't even be there.

I think back to when I was in my early thirties; I must say those were truly some of the greatest years of my life. If you are in your twenties, hang on, those years can often be a tough place; I call it the place of the "unknown". All of a sudden, all you thought you were trained for, all the years before, is thrown at you, and you now have to figure life out on your own. Maybe what you thought you wanted to do and be just isn't your passion anymore. Maybe the doors of opportunity seem to open for everyone else but you, and you find yourself comparing where you are to where someone else is, and you feel isolated. It can become a place of insecurity because those dreams we wrote about in our journal of what we wanted are now nothing like we thought, Sometimes just getting a job is tough, and now you have that degree, and now what do I do with it? I will get more into this later as I share my heart about Caleb. But hang in there. The thirties come quickly.

I knew who I was in my thirties as much as I possibly could, or at least I thought, and life was good. We moved out of our first home, and now we moved even further away from my husband's job. It seemed as if it was out in the country, cow pastures everywhere. Why in the world, Rhonda, did you decide to go look out further from the city when my husband already has so far to drive? Matt fell in love with it also; it was those five swimming pools, the golf community, the playgrounds, the parents walking with strollers, it all just sucked us in. But more importantly, now and once again, I know why. Here in a picturesque subdivision hidden in the hills of Acworth, Georgia, I would say the root of who I really am, now began here.

The book, the good juicy stuff, the laughter, the growth period, relationships, the questions, and the sorrow… indeed the stuff you don't plan for, the stuff moms don't dream of when we write in our private journals, these are the stories no one wants to talk about, the uncomfortable things that touch too deeply at the heart. I remember as a little girl having a little diary with the little locket on the side. I would write things about what I want for Christmas or my fears that seemed so big, like being afraid of the dark. Now the diary holds so much more; it holds life experiences that have formed who I am now; the pages have tear stains on them, smears of mascara where I have wiped my eyes and continued to write.

As I write this chapter, I truly have to give thanks to my mom. She was and continues to be my role model. Actually, I am blessed to have had women in my life that have been godly examples and have lived out experiences of pain and sorrow by continuing to praise God in the midst. And yet, as I am grateful for that, I know many of you haven't had that relationship with your mom; you've had to grow up without that in your life. Many of you have lost your mom through cancer, disease, and the longing for her advice; her love and relationship are deep. I don't take what I have for granted, and I cover you in prayer. You see, this book isn't just about my story, it's about you. It's about what we all face and go through; it's about the deep parts that no one really wants to talk about. It's the hours we lay in bed with our head on the pillow and tears fall. It's the times we've questioned, "what is my purpose"? The times when everyone seems to have their life together, and I can barely brush my teeth. Yes, those moments.

So, why do we try to keep up? Why do we try to be something we aren't and never will be? I know as a woman, I want to do what makes me feel valued; I want to do something that makes me feel I am making a difference. And yet sometimes, while we are trying to keep up, we are really falling apart. It's in our nature to long for the words to be heard like "I love you, and you are beautiful, I appreciate you, you are valuable to me." We wouldn't be human if we didn't want to hear these things. It's when we allow ourselves to base our confidence on those words that it becomes unhealthy.

My life was good, like I said, but looking back, I see I was wanting to make it perfect, and there was no way I could. I am not God. I cannot fix someone else, let alone myself, without His grace.

We moved to our new home, and I thought switching Caleb and Mackenzie from private school to public was the hardest thing I would deal with. It is all such a part of learning as a parent because we grow into our lives; we aren't already there. It's like a farmer who plants the seeds that may seem easy, but you have to water, take care of the soil, and then pray the harvest is good. So much of what we often feel and do can be from what we have experienced.

Now that I am older, I realize a lot of me was trying to "control situations and fix" things, and that comes from my childhood. We had what seemed to be the "perfect, church going, nice house, suburban family". Yet, it fell apart and quickly. Everything about what I had known up until the age of 13 had fallen apart, and all of a sudden, we were in a situation where I was now aware that my mom struggled to make ends meet. Many times, food was scarce, it was a privilege to have paper towels (now I realize I can't stand it when we are running low). We didn't have the luxury of having the heater or air on whatever was comfortable; when I say we dug for change, we dug for change.

I always felt loved and cared for. I just had to worry more about things that I shouldn't have had to at my age. Did I blame or hate my dad? No, I didn't. I never want any of my habits or insecurities to continue to be blamed on my past. That's the problem, if we don't deal with it, then we continue to have an excuse for our behavior. I don't want an excuse; I am one of many who have been disappointed with our childhood; I also am one of many who have chosen not to become the victim.

The circumstances of my childhood did, however, make me want more; I didn't want my children ever to be concerned about provision. If Matt and I were tight on money, it wasn't their job to worry about it.

I didn't care about keeping up with the HOMES, having the biggest and best of cars; I seriously just wanted our little world to be happy and healthy. I wanted others to know we are a happy family and our home to be a place people would find joy and comfort.

Then the teenage years began to come, and oh how quickly they appear. How can these beautiful, dependent, tooth missing, round cheeks with innocent questions so suddenly become long-legged, braces, and clumsy loud strangers in our home? Where was I when Caleb grew legs so long that they hung over the bed and had stretch marks from growing so quickly? How did it happen? When did he begin to question the "why's" of life? The questions of why can't I see the movie, why did that person that loved Jesus die? All of a sudden, the questions weren't so cute like they were when he was five. They were becoming hard questions I wasn't able to answer without a few heart palpitations, and many I could never answer because I didn't have the answers. Questions do get harder. I question things all the time, and sometimes there is no answer that's visible or can be googled.

I really felt I was doing all the right things, yet I failed and continue to do so. We were a part of a church my mom and her husband (my other dad) pastored, and although small, I can say my kids were surrounded with the teachings of Jesus, there were many activities, and they didn't have a choice if they wanted to be in the church play or not; it was a family church, and you are going to be in the play. They were covered and always with us, they were surrounded by love, and oh, the memories we made together helped to form our faith and strength as a family. We didn't need to have community groups as it was small enough that we were the community. Church picnics, birthday parties, prayer meetings, worship practice, Sunday School, it was way more powerful than I realized. I probably didn't appreciate it as I do now because back then, it was a lot of work. We would load the audio equipment every Sunday in our car; Matt would set it up, I would lead the worship practice, help in the youth group, and leave fulfilled but exhausted

I am going to be really honest in this book, and you may or may not like it, but I wish I wouldn't have sweat the small things, like when I battled with Caleb over "Pokémon" cards. I felt they were bad at the time when really, they weren't at all. I had just heard from someone else who thought that and went with their issue on it. He would cry as all the other friends had them, and he wanted to be a part of this newfound craze. I began to research and make my own decision and found out they weren't harmful at all; they weren't Tarot cards or witchcraft—just a bunch of cards with little alien-looking creatures that they would exchange with one another. So, I beg you to learn from my mistakes, research things for yourself, pray, and just trust your gut instinct. Don't try to keep up with what other moms, dads, or what others are saying. I truly believe most of the time, the mom's intuition is right on, and when my intuition was wrong, I was the first to apologize. Now there were things I would fight hard for that I knew no matter what everyone else said or did, I wouldn't give in to my child about. We have to have our own convictions even it isn't the popular thing to have.

Motherhood is hard; being a mom for the first time is a constant navigating, trying to find our way, the right way, and someone else's way may not be the right way for you. I wonder what would happen if we truly began not only to pray that we can make it through motherhood without too many issues but began to pray and empower other moms walking through it also.

So many times, I will hear about what some young person is doing, the mistake they made, and the label put on them. It's so wrong; it is our job to love them, disciple them, and lead them the right way. Spreading gossip and hurting a child is no way to make leaders. We must remember we all make mistakes. Let's get to their heart before the mistake has a big price to pay.

Everything I thought would one day matter, like the highest grades, the right college, the awards at school, the popular kids, and on and on, now no longer matters. Think back to your kids if they are older, and you will see most of what we worried about and compared our kids to now does not even matter. I find the ones we thought we were competing with are just trying to navigate their own lives, and no one is too concerned anymore if the other is ahead or not.

I often ask God to forgive me; my thoughts at times can wander and seem so shallow. I just envision God right beside me, shaking His head, saying, "Oh Rhonda, you are one funny lady." I remember as my kids began these middle school ages, just wanting them to know they were loved and accepted. Parents, if you are dealing with this age, please know you aren't alone. I am praying for you. This age is hard, it's tough, it's not so pretty, and so we need one another. Don't be afraid to confide in someone you can trust to share what you are dealing with. We are all in this together, and if I can be there for you, I will be. I am going to be honest because I sure failed; even with all I thought I was doing right, I would make many mistakes. Thankful for a God who loves me when my parenting skills fail.

Caleb wasn't one who struggled with being loved; he was easy to love, easy to communicate with, easy to become a part of the surroundings socially. He made it easy in that way for me. I never heard anything negative from his teachers, except he talked too much. He never was afraid to enter the unknown, whether it be a new school, or classroom, or a sport that he was new at. He fit in easily, and maybe that could have been a strength and a weakness at the same time.

I remember sitting in the car line after school and looking for the tall blonde guy who was making everyone laugh. Sometimes it was exhausting for me; his mind was always thinking of what he could do that was funny. One day he decided to do the Greek Celebration off of my porch with plates and screamed "OPRAH," not the traditional word but his version. He cleaned it up, so no worries, but he was always coming up with something hilarious. I reflect on things he did, and as I write, I smile. Sometimes at those beginning teenage years, I would be disciplining so calmly and feeling confident in my conversation with him and then found myself laughing because he would do something so funny, yet there were many tears. He would cry when he knew he was disappointing us; he would always ask for forgiveness and quickly. Caleb had one of the most tender hearts, a desire to please God and others. I remember how we would share God's grace and forgiveness, and as much as we love Caleb, He loved him more. He wrestled with how God could love us in all of our yuck. I wrestled with how I could even begin to show him the love God has for him when it's so pure and so deep, hard to imagine that God loved Caleb as much as I did, and yet… He does.

Now at the age of 52, as I end this chapter, I realize I have no competition left in me, no first-place trophy, no best mom award, no national title, and nothing that could compare to knowing that my heart is right with God. I can't race beside you or anyone else. I can't pretend to have it all together only to reveal I am, at times, falling apart. I find it easy to be honest with you, my friends, and yes, I would say it to your face, I fail, I die daily, but for His Grace.

I see your little fingerprints everywhere I look, on the windows, on the walls, and even in your books.

I try to wipe away these prints, but they won't disappear, for as I try to wipe them off, I seem to wipe my tears.

This was written one day when the kids were all little, and the sliding glass door was covered in tiny fingerprints, and I knew then I would one day miss this, and yes, I wiped a tear.

Let's Just Eat Popcorn and Watch a Movie

Oh, how I long for those days, I talk about them all the time. I even find myself reliving those special moments, the smells, the laughter, the warmth of family. As parents, I think we all agree full-blown play days are the best. I love the days where they come in exhausted, smelling like puppies, and hungry for dinner. Those are the days I knew they were fulfilled, it was bath time and cozy pajamas, dinner, and then we would seal the night with popcorn and a movie. I knew I loved those moments then, but I know I would appreciate them even more now. It was as if Jesus Himself was sitting right beside us watching the Disney movie and saying, "Yes, it was a really good day."

Then the flu would come, the virus, ear infections, and birthday parties that exhausted us all, but although exhausting, it seems so easy now. Baseball games, dance lessons, basketball games, early morning practices, and yet I wouldn't trade those days for anything. I found magic with my kids during those young years; the Disney Store at the mall was something we all looked forward to. We would come home with a costume just because coming home with toys that my kids didn't need, yet it was just fun and sweet and everything good in a candy store.

But we all know, life is life. As long as we are human and on earth, there will be problems, sickness, failure, and grief. When I was young, the word grief meant it was something that happened only to older people. When I was in high school, very rarely did you hear about the deaths of young people; I didn't feel bombarded by competition or sorrow. It seemed my friends and I were just concerned with what we would wear to school and who would take us to the mall. The way life should be, right? Kids shouldn't have to face cancer, disease, mental illness, loss. I imagine the picture we all have seen of Jesus sitting down, and all the young children gathered around him with smiles on their faces. Shouldn't it be that way here on earth? Why do we face such deep sorrow? Why do the questions haunt us of why?

I remember someone so very dear to me lost her son at a young age. I remember crying with her over the phone. I remember the funeral, and I wondered how she was able to stand and greet the hundreds of people wanting to console them. I said to myself, "God, please don't ever let anything happen to my children. I wouldn't make it."

Now, this doesn't mean anything whatsoever is going to happen to your child; it just means I think as parents, we all say that. How would I face such deep sorrow? We aren't created to live in a place of "what ifs".

> For God has not given us a spirit of fear, but of power and of love and of a sound mind.
>
> —2 Timothy 1:7 NKJV

The word of God clearly speaks that over us. I oftentimes find myself going over and over it in my mind. Sometimes I imagine just the powerful words written on my forehead like a tattoo, and I see it there to cover my mind with positive, powerful words.

We can't possibly understand why bad things happen in life, why the God we serve and who loves us allows such deep sorrow to invade. And yet, I know in the midst of the storm, He is there. He is as there as the air we breathe, we don't see it, but we trust in it.

It's almost a guarantee that being a parent will have ups and downs, happy times, tears, and the movie and the popcorn idea that the kids used to love won't quite sound as good to them as taking the car out for the evening with their friends and going to a movie that we don't approve of. Yup, that could be another book in itself.

It happens so quickly; it honestly does. Don't you feel you are changing their diapers one minute, the next they are changing their moods every second? Mood swings go on a whole new level during those tween and teenage years. We truly can't prepare for this as a parent; we have no idea what transpires from the child who went to bed in their footed pajamas and woke up in boxer shorts.

I look around as I see these teenagers, and I just start to pray for them and for their parents. I was there just a few years ago, not too long ago, and I realize we need all the prayer we can get; being a parent is not an easy job. We need to quit judging each other and instead maybe reach out and share experiences, what worked for us when we were dealing with this age. I also have a very special heart for the single parents who have to carry this alone. I watched my mom do it. She would work and try to play both roles, and somewhere along the journey, you realize you can't be both. I support you, moms and dads, you may feel alone, but you aren't. You may not know, but there are those who are watching you drop them off at school, watching as you manage to make it to their activities, although exhausted, God is aware of how much you give up for yourself so they can have it. I relate because I grew up in a single-parent home; I watched all my mom gave up so we could have more.

There are seasons of life we all must go through, and I am not speaking of just the natural order of life, but as the spring season of life, the fresh season of new hope and change. Then the summer seasons are a time where it's usually full of rest and God's awesome beauty. We have the fall season of life where things begin to change, the smell of fall is in the air, and the beautiful colors, and we sense God's provision and harvest. Then the winter season comes, and we can start to feel the barren season.

Then there is this winter season of life; nothing seems beautiful, the skies are gray, and hang low, the trees are no longer full of color, and the leaves have fallen. And yet, this is usually the season in my life God shows up the most. It's the season I am digging deep in me to see what it is I need to do to produce a harvest, what I need to change in me so that I can find joy in the midst of this season of life. Although the winter season of my life can be so very hard with all the holidays, birthdays, and tragic dates and reminders, I don't want to skip over this season because, in this season, I grew and continue to grow.

I felt life even when death was at my door. Life seriously is beautiful; in my grief, I still love life, I still love people, I love even more than I did before Caleb died. Is it all popcorn and movies at home with the kids all safe and cozy? No, but that was a season I will forever treasure, and if you are in this season with your kids, I am celebrating with you and would like to be invited over. It's a great time of life that I believe God so graciously gives us.

He has bestowed upon us good and beautiful things, he has given us hope, he gives us a place of rest for our weariness, and in all the yuck he is changing us, I would never have had this strength and trust in him had I not gone through this and been prepared years before by trusting in even the little things.

Many of those tests of faith came through what others were facing in my family. When I say "close" family, we always have been. We have pretty much always lived close by or lived together, or we were crying because we felt too far away from each other. I was the middle child, my brother Kevin was the oldest, and Gina was the baby sister. The memories we shared even as little ones were wonderful. I honestly don't remember a time we weren't close. Maybe when my brother went through his teenage years, and I wasn't there quite yet. I didn't understand him, and he didn't understand me, but we really didn't even fight other than the normal things that brothers and sisters fight over, usually just them annoying us. There may have been a time I was curling my hair with hot rollers and threw one at him after he aggravated me over and over. Having an older brother does teach you to fight back, so thanks, Kevin.

So, we grew up together, and we watched Little House on the Prairie and the Walton's and ate popcorn that you had to pop on the stove, and so that became a place of safety. We became adults with grown-up responsibilities but so grateful that life still kept us in the same vicinity but all with different stories.

Then the words "cancer" hit our family and way too close to home. My sister was diagnosed with stage 3 breast cancer when her youngest daughter was only one year old. The doctor didn't seem to sugar coat anything, go home and get things in order were the harsh words from the doctor. That doctor didn't last long, and we found one that had a plan and brought words of hope to her instead of death. Life changed suddenly, and the sick to the stomach feeling of "what if" invaded us all.

I watched my sister fight this battle and sing in the midst of che-mo. She wrote songs and had a CD come out with all songs she wrote during her battle. She would come to church and look beautiful with her wigs on. She was a mom and didn't want to miss a thing and be a part of it all, take care of her two little girls and fight, and God healed her, and she stands fifteen years later, cancer-free and a miracle. That season of life wasn't always sunny with no chance of rain, there were days the thunderstorms came, and fear poured upon us all, but the sun came out again, and I call it God's Grace, the rainbow of His promise was always revealed, and hope was given.

We were thrilled to see what God had done, and my mom had her daughter, and she was alive, and all was well.

Not too many years after this, my brother Kevin, whose daughter Hanna at the time was ten, was diagnosed with lymphoma. I know this must be wrong; this cannot be happening again, really God.? I watched my mom go through this with my sister and now her son? God, where are you in this? What kind of God would allow this to happen again? Yes, we can ask those questions; I promise you this, He can handle it.

But seriously, how much more could we handle. I hated seeing the pain my mom was going through. Kevin was very sick and fought back with chemo and radiation and did all he could do, and for a year, he was in remission. He was vibrant and looked better than ever. He was able to treasure this year with his daughter. Oh, how he fought to live for her. Looking back now, I see God was aware and allowed this time for him, and this season of healing to be a testimony of what God had done for his life. He was full of gratitude and hope. But the season ended, and he lost his battle to cancer. Death thought it won, but that day as we stood around his bedside and worshipped, I watched as he took his last breath and seriously saw the face of Jesus literally come and take over his face. Jesus entered that room and took Kevin to a place of no more suffering, no more sickness, a place where he can fish all day, a place of rest. It showed me that heaven is real when I saw Jesus in that room; I felt His presence so strong it was a heavenly moment. This wasn't a moment that a movie could script up perfectly, it was a divine moment, and peace flooded the home, yes sorrow, but not despair, for we knew he was free and would suffer no more. After seeing Kevin die and what transpired, it confirmed in me all I had been taught from a young child about Jesus; He brings peace, and Heaven is real.

I won't go into all the details, but soon after, my dad was diagnosed with cancer and died three years later. I was able to watch my dad worship in his bed and sing to the Lord. He continued to have faith and continued to speak God's word. All the failures and disappointments that we had with our father didn't matter anymore; we knew his heart; we knew he loved us. God, I am so very grateful for those special times where my sister and I would sing with him, take him to the doctor and watch him believe. We also knew he was ready to be with Jesus, no more suffering for my dad either, but I don't want to lose one more person. As we know, they aren't suffering, they are at peace; it is our broken hearts here on earth that ache for them. It was 2010 and 2013, the years that two people I loved dearly were gone from our lives, and the seasons weren't full of harvest and overflowing with joy; no these seasons were tough, and we often wondered how much more could we take.

And yet I promise this; God continued to show up. Miracles continued to happen, hope began to unveil itself in beautiful ways, in beautiful people, and more importantly, we realized we couldn't do life without His grace. You will read about that word a lot in my book, and it's because it's so real to me, and I guess you could say the word that keeps me going, and I promise you this, it will sustain you also. GRACE, not the thing we say at mealtime but the grace that allows you to awaken in the morning and get out of bed when life is unfair; grace is the power you are given to walk into situations that seem unbearable. It sustains; it allows us to grieve but not without hope.

So, today this morning, as I am writing this, it's actually pouring outside, but I want you to know if you are in a season of hopelessness that as you read this, you can rest in knowing God is right beside you, there is someone praying for you, there are people who love you. Don't carry this alone; make your requests known to God, share with a friend you can trust, reach out for help.

I promise you will have a time again for popcorn, a cozy blanket, and a movie. It will feel good again, maybe not like it used to, but there will be peace and moments of joy. Your circumstances may be different, but the sun will peek through the heavy clouds, and you will find a smile on your face. Hold on.

… My grace is sufficient for you, for my power is made perfect in weakness.

—2 Corinthians 12:9 ESV

The Day My Earth Stood Still

It was a typical day in February, overcast and chilly, not freezing but just enough sun to peek through a mostly cloudy day.

A day I awoke taking all for granted, a day of the "unexpected," a day that would change our lives forever, a day that would cause us to breathe differently, a day hearts truly were broken, and a day we will mark as the day we were forced to live life differently, a day that changed my dependency on God.

It's funny how you look back at a major event, whether good or bad, happy or tragic, and you see things that happened prior to it. Maybe they could have been warning signs, words from God, or just affirmations to let you know you were loved, this is completely normal because I would say we aren't prepared, or we would live in a state of fear. We shouldn't be prepared for great loss; we shouldn't be anticipating something awful. But now I look back and say, "Wow, God, you brought all this to remind me that YOU were aware."

At the time, I worked in this adorable store, full of beautiful things that women love; clothes, jewelry, house decor, and so much more. I didn't realize at the time why I was taking this job. Yes, of course, the money would help, but to be honest, it wasn't going to pay a house payment, but every bit helps. But it was a time the kids were older, and Micah was driving himself, and now I had extra time, and why not hang with fun people and look at the beauty all around me. I didn't realize that day on 2-10-2016 as I waited on someone who lost someone dear to them to cancer that a few hours later, I would be faced with death. As I helped her find an outfit, I felt myself hurting for her and their family. She was a beautiful woman, and I could see her heart was hurting, the loss was great and raw, and her spirit was so tender. She left, and I prayed.

I walked the store that day and around 2:00 p.m. and all of a sudden, I stopped, and I remember exactly where it was and said, "Wow, life is good for me right now, Thank you, Jesus." We had a fun vacation with all the family planned the following week. Caleb was excited, a week out of school and time to eat all day and fish. Mackenzie was in a good place in LA, and Micah was pretty much the easiest child so far, and my husband was anticipating a much needed time away at the beach. We didn't care whether we would have beach weather; we were excited about a home we rented where we all could be together, laugh, eat, play games, talk, ride bikes. This would be a good week, but little did I know. A reminder to me of how we can plan for the perfect vacation, we can pack the perfect outfits, save money for time to be together. I visualized us all playing games around the table, all of us dancing in the kitchen while we would cook dinner. I could see us all falling asleep on the couch while watching a movie and moments full of deep conversation. These were our "vacation" moments, and I couldn't wait for this date to come.

It was time for work to be over, and 3:00 p.m. approached, and work had ended for the day, just a few errands and home I would be with Matt and Micah. I remember driving, thinking, *Wow, I didn't get an 11:00 am call or text from Caleb*, but normally I would have realized that before while at work, but for some reason that day, I just felt peace. I remember driving and at the red light realizing his text I had sent wasn't going through. I think we all know that panic feeling when it's not "delivered". I began to feel the knots in the stomach, but there had to be a reason; Caleb was so good about communication. I called his number that is so memorized in my mind, and it goes straight to voicemail. I called again, straight to voicemail. I felt the knots getting stronger; fear began to invade.

This is hard to write, I have started and stopped more times than I can count. I have reread it over and over, and it doesn't get easier. The feelings and the knot in the stomach return, no matter how long it has been.

Before I go further, I want to tell you a little more about Caleb. It doesn't mean when your child doesn't respond immediately that something is wrong, quite possibly their phone is dead. But anyone who knows Caleb, knows he is a communicator. As a mom, a mom knows their child and their patterns. He would text throughout the day or call; he would want to discuss plans for the day, things he was worried or excited about, and many times wanted to know if we could meet for lunch. Caleb often communicated to me about things that were hard to digest as a mom; he was respectful (usually), but I often would say, "Caleb, I don't need to know this." Caleb wasn't good at hiding his flaws, his fears, his mistakes. Caleb was one who believed more in everyone else than he did himself. But he loved family, he loved his friends, and I know he loved his mama. I will have more on who he was later on, and in every chapter, you will sense his personality and gain maybe understanding of who you are, your child, or just get to know this incredible person, our Caleb.

It's crazy because as I write, I relive the smells, the air, the smothering of fear I felt as I started driving to what was supposed to be the dry cleaners, but just kept going straight. At least I could be closer to him as I drove. I called his roommate, who immediately answered, "Could you please check on Caleb? He isn't answering."

He replied so innocently, not knowing what he would face, "Sure, I just got home from work, let me check." "He isn't breathing; he isn't breathing. NOOOOOOOOOO… CALL 911 NOW!"

I sensed the panic in his voice and hated he was the one who was put in this situation. I called my husband, no answer. My heart felt heavy. I don't know what I was doing or how I was even driving. Finally, I find myself heading towards 75 S as Caleb lived about 30 minutes away, but it was 3:30 p.m., and traffic was starting to get bad. "Matt, ANSWER, please God, please God, this is just a dream, it's all a dream!"

You see, death doesn't care if you are in the busiest season of your life, if you have a family vacation planned next week, if you are driving in the car alone when you hear the words that speak death over you. Death doesn't care.

The words I spoke came quickly and loud when my husband answered. "MATT, CALEB'S NOT BREATHING, HE'S NOT BREATHING!" He knew it wasn't some kind of joke. I felt the panic in his voice. I feel I felt his heartbeat through the phone. "I'm on my way," he said. Then the sound of dial tone. In between all this, I couldn't remember how to get to Caleb's apartment. I couldn't remember anything. Just screaming alone in the car, panicking, and yet trying to get a hold of my family to get to Micah, so he can have someone with him, the mom mode was kicking in full gear, and yet I wasn't ready to face what was possibly lying ahead of me either. I couldn't quite think of everyone that needed to be taken care of. "Please, please just let this be a dream, a misunderstanding. This doesn't make sense to me."

Images of what I could face were flashing through my mind, all while screaming on the phone to my husband I don't know how to get there, I don't remember. Agonizing red lights that seemed to last forever, the slow drivers had no idea why I anxiously wanted to pass them. I needed to get to my son… I needed to save him… to be the one to comfort him… I need to get there now. I felt if I can just get to him, he would breathe again, life would be as normal. *This is all a mistake…*

I am sure someone noticed me screaming in my car as they sat next to me at the lights. I am sure they had to be aware of something was wrong. "God, are you listening to me? I need you to help Caleb. Please, God, PLEASE!" As moms, our minds never stop even when life does seem to be peaceful. We are constantly thinking of the next thing on our list, how to make our children happy, the house needs cleaned, the bills need paid. All while not wanting to believe my son was dead, my mind was already thinking of how I would tell my daughter and son, my mom, my family. Oh yes, I believed there was hope, but something told me to prepare for the worst. You don't prepare for the worst when it's your child. No, only for yourself; we prepare to leave for vacation, get a will done, sign someone to have guardianship if something happens to us as parents. No, I don't prepare for losing a child. We don't buy extra life insurance to pay for our child's funeral. This is all wrong, backward, crazy, this isn't my life.

All I know is, I wanted to get to my son, but yet inside, I didn't know if I was ready to face it. Who is, though? you don't come prepared for unexpected deaths, loss. If we did, we would live in fear. I remember getting to the gate and having no way in. The young lady in front looked at me as if she knew, "Are you here with the ambulances?" "Yes, it's my son." She looked as if she already knew and let me in. The car couldn't stop fast enough as I pulled into the space where he lived; this isn't his place. Ambulance, cops, and the evident... death was at the door.

Matt had a look I have never seen in his eyes, a look I never want to see again and words I can never hear again, "He's gone, he's gone." As I write, I am reliving the heartbeat that seemed to pound out of my chest, I at that moment, knew what a broken heart was. Not the kind of broken heart of your first love breakup, not the kind of hurt when you hear your parents are divorcing, or painful hurts of life. No, the heartbreak that you know can never be repaired here on earth, the kind you never dreamed would be yours to live with. The kind of hurt that nothing in the world could replace... nothing.

The air was smothering. The clouds were low and heavy as I sat in my car... waiting... as Matt went to see if he could see our son... I felt the air in my lungs being sucked out of me. How can I breathe? I won't make it through this if this is real. The heaviness Matt was carrying already trying to be strong for me, but this was his son also, his firstborn, and we couldn't save him. As a matter of fact, we weren't allowed to see him that day. With deep condolences, they told us, "You don't want to see your son this way." What way? Cold, blue, lifeless... —not the tall, loud, powerful, strong, hilarious, handsome Caleb? Where is that Caleb? We wanted to walk up there and have God breathe life back into him, and we wanted it now. I had enough love and faith to do that at that moment, but yet I knew, oh indeed, I knew. Our son was gone.

If ever adrenaline flooded me, it was at this moment. I felt I was going full speed, and yet time stood still. As I write this, I know exactly my movements, my thoughts. You see, this kind of death is a tough place to go back to. That is why this book is so hard to write because it's the real deal. It isn't a Nicholas Sparks book, where usually it all ends well. There is nothing but real truth in this story, real characters living out the pains and the screams of sorrow. The rainbow didn't appear that day of hope; no, the clouds hung low that day, February 10th, 2016.

Social media scared me even greater on this day because my fear was the word would get out through his friends that lived there before I could get to my family. My sister, the breast cancer survivor, the fighter who fought to live, could now help me get to my youngest son and my mom. I needed a warrior, and she was it. Micah was in tenth grade driving home from school that day, and that can be scary in itself. I couldn't picture him finding out and having to drive home. Mackenzie was twenty and living in Los Angeles. *How in the world can I tell them? How?*

I can't even let the words resonate within myself. How do I speak these words of death and yet let my kids know hope is still here? How do I speak life to them when death has knocked on the home of their heart? I had to get to Mackenzie in California. California was three hours behind Georgia, and I knew she would soon see something on social media, and I couldn't let the world tell her she has lost and lost deeply. I called her friends, who had to call other friends to get to her. I couldn't call her directly; someone had to be with her. I remember her friends answering, and with apprehension, I heard them say "Hello" as if to say, *why are you calling me?* I could even hear the waves crashing as they said, "Yes, Mackenzie is here at Malibu beach with us." Was it the waves, or was it the crashing of all I thought was good in my life?

"There has been a horrible loss, and we need you to be with Mackenzie as we talk to her."

Mackenzie has a very soft voice, and this day it seemed even softer. "Mom, hey, I am at the beach. It is so beautiful today. Can I call you later"?

"Oh, Kenzie, I have something to tell you; it's not good, Kenzie. Caleb has died; he's gone." The silence, the moans, the screams still invade my thoughts.

"Mom, stop; it's not funny, this isn't real."

Her screams didn't sound like she was thousands of miles away, they were so loud, and even visually, I could picture her face. "We will make it, Kenzie, we will make it."

"Mom, no, no, no, you have to stop, he will make it, he will live." The groans seemed as if she was right next to me, yet I couldn't hold her, I couldn't comfort, I couldn't let her fall into my arms and hold her tight and wipe the tears from her eyes. I could do nothing, absolutely nothing, but barely breathe. And yet, this thing called grace to sustain appeared.

Chaos was everywhere. My somewhat peaceful world was now a mess. Gina, my sister, is at my home telling my baby boy Micah his brother is gone. How do you explain that without yourself crumbling to the floor in despair? The groans that came out of Micah should never have to be from your child; the tears should never have to fall so quickly; the sounds of death should never be heard in this way. The sounds of death, the smell of death was everywhere we were; it was a nightmare, and I still thought maybe I would wake up, yet this quickly became our new life.

Pounding on the dashboard, screaming, "THIS CANNOT BE. I WANT MY CALEB. I WANT MY SON!" Traffic, bumper to bumper, and no one cared to get out of our way. They were worried they wouldn't be home for dinner in time. They had to get to their son's game, get to the bar to drown their sorrows. I just wanted to get home and bury myself in my families' arms, lay on the floor, and scream, "God, Why, WHY, WHY, WHY?"

I can even remember how it felt walking to the door of my home, looking up as my family stood on the porch weeping with arms wide open. I remember it so vividly. I will share with you, and I won't leave out details because it wasn't an episode and series on Netflix or Lifetime. This has been a chapter I haven't been able to write. I put off writing this book, especially this part, as I knew it would come in painfully raw again. These kinds of emotions go deep again and again and again. I couldn't write it until today. I have trained my mind to only go to this day and only go to certain parts because it's too sickening. No, I am not healed, so don't look for my book on healing and a miracle. It doesn't happen that way when a child dies, but yes, oh yes, indeed, I will share on the abundance of grace that covered us and still does. I will share on the hope that only comes from knowing who our eternal Father was and the promise of being with Caleb again.

But this day, a day many parents have experienced, was a day like none other. A day you don't want to revisit, but yet you have to because it's now a part of your life, your story, your heart, the makeup now of your "whys" of life. My husband began to make the calls as I heard him weep in his office. I don't know how I functioned that night. I remember moaning all night, five minutes of sleep here and there, and jolting off the couch screaming. Matt never changed his clothes; his shoes still on his feet, the shoes that carried such sorrow as the weight of the world was now upon Matt. We didn't sleep soundly for months, and this night was the beginning of what I call "Midnight Hours". The hours where darkness not only literally invades, but darkness tries to bury us with the reality of death. And yet, the sun came up the next morning, and the clouds still hung low, the sounds of death still lingering loudly in our home as more family arrived, friends, neighbors, and soon my girl would arrive from LA after an overnight flight. Micah was covered with friends but never left my side until he knew it was okay; Mom would be okay. You aren't just in pain for yourself, but to see your family in pain and yet you know they have to live it as you are, you can't bandage it, you can't take a trip to Target to make it better, no this isn't even a surgery where in time it will just be a scar, it's a scar of the heart. From the outside, all may seem whole, and unless you know the story, all may seem beautiful. Until you know them, you don't know.

Mackenzie arrived with her friends holding her up, her eyes almost swollen shut, her tall body looking too weak to stand. Collapsing in each other's arms seemed to become the normal for all of us. When one was stronger, the other would collapse; when was weaker, the other became the pillar. At that moment, I think we both collapsed, and we were held together by others. This wasn't supposed to be; she was supposed to come home and have dinner with all of us. Caleb was supposed to be making all of us laugh and playing us a new song. Caleb doesn't make everyone cry; that's not who he was, who he is, that's not normal; this isn't normal. I would describe one thing about death; it's as if you are living outside of your body. You feel you aren't really "present," yet how can it be when the pain is so evident. It's a feeling like none other and one no one should ever have to experience.

Now, it was time to plan. Day two and already having to plan a funeral, the words kept ringing loudly as grief kept coming through the door. Yes, grief came through the door in people of all ages, colors, and sizes. Our political views didn't matter, our race, our relationship, stepmoms, stepdads, distant relatives, it didn't matter, grief didn't care; it entered all of us. It came quickly, no warning, and now we all were left to deal with the outcome of one bad decision.

People from everywhere entered our home. I remember getting out of bed to go to the kitchen and was barely able to move, people sitting on the floors, the dining room so full of people and food that I didn't even recognize my home. I did, though, recognize "Grief". I recognized the look in their eyes and the words that would say, "I am so sorry," as I would often fall in their arms, or maybe for a brief moment have enough strength to tell them "I am sorry" and let them fall on me. The moans as new people would enter were loud, then you would hear silence, and everyone seemed to whisper. At times I wanted to scream, "TALK LOUD, THIS ISN'T REAL, BE NORMAL." And yet, as the hours progressed and the darkness set in, night two was a reminder that death had come, and it wasn't going to change.

Evenings would set in, and you could hear the television on, and for some reason, it brought some sense of normality to our home. Until the moment, the commercial would have a song, a melody, a reminder, and we couldn't silence the volume quickly enough. Even the television echoed our pain. It was the evident, and again I will say, the evident was missing.

How many of you prepare for a funeral for your child? They are healthy, beginning the prime of their life. It's not on the to-do list that today while on the way to the grocery store, let me go pick out my sons' gravesite and casket. Let me make sure I have enough in the bank to cover his funeral should he die. No, I don't think that way, and neither did my husband. This wasn't something I could even write with a pen of "Just in case of emergency". No, not a chance any of my children will die before I do. And yet, right now, we were dealing with the day he would have his viewing, the day of the funeral.

Day Three, the day my husband had to confirm this was our son, lying on a stretcher at the funeral home. I heard the cries of our son Micah who wanted to go see him with his dad. I sat in the lobby, not quite ready for this, or will I ever be? I can answer that now, no you never are ready for this. That's where the abundance of grace comes in. Yes, I will speak so much on this word because it sustains us; it covers us. Sometimes it may feel like the blanket that isn't quite long enough to cover your feet when stretched out on the couch, and yet you want them covered and your upper body also, and you stretch and stretch for it to cover all of you. Somehow it just keeps stretching and not full coverage but enough to warm you. That's what grace does, the pain is still there and grace can't take that away, but He gives us enough to give us strength; the blanket may feel small and much of what is revealed is cold and painful, but somehow, it keeps us warm enough to make it.

As long as we are here on earth, we will never not have pain; that's the reality of life, of sin, of what changed at the very beginning of God's plan. Just one sin changed the plan of the world.

The blanket felt small; there was no way there could be enough grace to cover us, to even get us through to the next morning. AND YET, it did. Grace stretched over us, the pain was revealed; raw cold pain was revealed, but grace covered.

Day four, you are coming too fast and yet so slow. Too long since I have heard my son's voice, and too fast that I have to say goodbye to his physical body. I am asked what do I want him to wear, what do I want him to be in when people come to say their "goodbyes"? I am taken back to the day I brought him home from the hospital, carrying him, knowing he was the most valuable thing I had ever held at that point. He was breakable. I wrapped the clean new blanket around him tightly, swaddled him so he would feel safe and warm. I wanted to wrap Caleb up again, keep him safe, get him out of the wooden box, and take him home. Yes, the day I brought him home was joyous, and the day I am now facing is excruciating. I would find myself jolting out of thoughts, shaking my head to get my mind clear, yet it was racing full speed ahead of what was and what will be. GOD HELP ME!

On this day, I was going through the motions, picking out clothes for Caleb, myself, and making sure we all are ready with the outward clothes because we know that's the only thing we can control at this time. The inward is a process, a process only God can deal with. In our own strength, we can barely get showered and dressed. The inward part is what God is working on, He's not leaving us. He's holding our hearts in the palm of His hand, and that's how we are breathing.

Day five the day of his viewing. The day I will see my son for the first time since last Monday, the day I will see him without breath in his lungs, with stillness in his body, with no voice saying, "Mom, I love you". Yes, today, I must face the biggest giant I have ever, ever faced—The giant of death, fear, sorrow, and pain—The giant that carries nothing but death in him, the giant that crushes hopes and dreams. Today, I will enter a room of tears, wails, and yet silence. It's approaching the hour in which I must get in the car and be driven to the place of "goodbyes". I feel as if I am walking, but on air, nothing underneath me to stabilize my fall, nothing to make me feel secure. I remember so clearly as I write this about the smells, the air, the sky, the temperature, the atmosphere was heavy yet so full of love for Caleb. In the midst of such great sorrow, I won't forget the amount of love that poured out.

As a family, we get to go in first and have our time alone with Caleb before anyone else comes in. We get to have our moment, our forever memory of him alone, just Matt, Mackenzie, Micah, me, and the giant of grief. How do you step in the door of the room that holds the body of your dead child? How do you approach grief that lies before your eyes to such an extent you may have to actually run away? We approach, I don't know, maybe it was slow motion, but it wasn't the eager walk or run to see your child and hug them when they pull up in the driveway after being away at school. It wasn't the anticipation when you wait at the bus stop and can't wait to see them step off and run to you. No, this is different; it's wanting to see him so bad, and yet none of this makes sense.

I remember the way he looked that day. Actually, he looked so handsome, as if he was just taking a nap after dinner, a look of peace with his cute little smile. He didn't look like death, yet his body was cold. Yes, I touched him. I kissed his lips; I rubbed his long fingers and his forehead. There was nothing weird about this; a mother's love will do anything to touch one more time, to hold one more time. I knew I wouldn't see him anymore, only in my dreams. As I write, I am frozen again because no matter how many times I live it out, say it, relive it, say it, I cannot believe my Caleb is gone. He's gone from this earth, and there isn't anything I can do, no prayer that will bring him back.

The viewing, however, is a love story to us. A love story of Caleb and how much he was loved by everyone. Wrapped around the building were hundreds of people, young people, old people, kids, parents, grandparents, teachers, cousins, aunts, uncles, people that never even met him but heard about him—hours upon hours of people coming and expressing their sorrow and love for us. The room was crowded, full of swollen eyes, broken hearts, broken lives, broken... broken... broken...

Our tall 6'4" son, so strong, lying in a casket... In the midst of this grief, we must tell you some funny things because that's what keeps life real. Yes, moments of laughter still come at the worst of times. I call them, "God's give me a break moment". When picking out the casket, they ask you how tall your child is. We knew he was 6'4", and you answer questions you never dreamed you would one day have to answer about your child? Really? These people in this industry amaze me; they are some of the kindest, most compassionate people on this planet, a place where they constantly have to console the grieving families and yet make sure their casket is correct. That's tough to balance, and they do so well. They so gently expressed to us that they are having a tough time fitting our son in the casket that he is measuring 6'6" and it would have to be a special ordered one.

At this point, we couldn't handle one more thing and our cousin Tarah was one that could help with decision making when we couldn't, and she said, "Do what you have to do, bend his knees, it has to work." Yes, we smiled amongst the anguish. This was just like Caleb to pull a little trick and surprise us. We knew he had looked taller lately but 6'6"? So many other little stories that we look back at and are able to laugh a bit.

My niece couldn't get her nose to stop bleeding, all while constantly saying, "Wow, Caleb had good looking friends." My other niece is lying down on the couch saying she's going to pass out, and the sink in the bathroom is overflowing because another family member is trying to heat a baby bottle. It was life, real life in the midst of a nightmare, and isn't it just like life can be? Wow, we can go back and look at situations we've all been through and find some humor in the moment, usually because of family and the funny things and the ins and outs we all know about each other's craziness. We need those moments to laugh, the moments that breathe a little bit of normalcy back into our lives, even if it's just for a brief second.

The day known around the world as Valentines' Day, the day of love, was the day hundreds gathered in a grief-filled room to come weep with us. Love wasn't supposed to hurt this deep. Love wasn't supposed to cause anguish of the soul, it's Valentines' Day, and I am at the viewing of my son. Life, you don't make sense sometimes, and right now, I am really not happy with you.

How will I awaken tomorrow and bury my son, how God?

I cried out to him with my head buried in my pillow, covered in blankets that couldn't warm the ache of my heart. I was covered in heartache that only the Comforter could comfort. If I don't awaken tomorrow, at least I will be with Caleb. Don't be shocked; I think every grieving parent has had that thought run through their mind, just for a moment to be reunited with our child and for the pain to leave. I made it through the night and the morning came. The sun barely rose, and the clouds were low. It's February, and it's not a beautiful month to begin with, then add the barrenness of our loss, and the clouds hung even lower; a gray that doesn't have any hints of green trees behind it, or a flower blooming in a field, just gray a painful gray. I don't even know how we all got dressed that day, the house was full of family and guests, and the table and kitchen continued to overflow with food. Food keeps life in a home, even if you don't eat it because you've lost your appetite. But it was good for me to hear the noise in the kitchen and, once in a while, hear a quiet laugh instead of the overwhelming moans of sorrow.

I would breathe in and out so deep; I felt my heart was pounding. Would I make it today? And yet, I had peace at times come and flood me, I felt strength pour through my veins and just enough to make it to the front row to sit with my husband, daughter, Micah, and I all laying with our heads on each other's shoulders. Micah never left my side, his arm constantly around me, as Mackenzie wept on her dad's shoulder and this was just the beginning of the service, how would we proceed. I couldn't look behind me or even beside me. I could only stare straight ahead at the wooden box with flowers displayed over plaid fabric, my son's picture on top. Guitars placed by the casket, everything was a perfect representation of who he is, except this shouldn't be, no, this shouldn't be. They say adrenaline kicks in to get you through these times, and indeed it does, but no amount of adrenaline could do what God does in these moments. Adrenaline didn't feel the room with God's presence. It was God himself. The comforter had come to us. It began with worship; it invaded the church, and before I could even think about it, as a family, we were all standing up in worship, arms outstretched in total surrender. There was no other way for our family to make it through without worship.

I think there are so many things you can't remember because it's a blur, but I remember so strongly the presence of God that day; we were bathed in grace and a sweet fragrance of His presence. Yes, grief can be in the same room as Jesus, and oh grief was evident in the swollen eyes, the heads hung low, the quivering lips, the heartbreak, but at the same time, hope was there because Jesus was in the room. We worshipped and listened to gifted talented family and friends sing and express their love for Caleb. Our hearts were full of God's presence, even in such an atmosphere of sorrow. How could these both be in the room at the same time?

We were honored to have Matt's brother Roger, who is a pastor at a church in CA, come and share. We knew how hard it was for him to speak while he knew his nephew was in a casket, and his brother sat weeping on the front row. The message was so what we needed to hear, and then John Carrette, my cousin's husband from Honduras who had mentored Caleb when he lived in Honduras and had been such a vital part of his life then spoke and shared about the grace of Jesus, all eyes were on him because all of us knew we needed a Savior. Matt and I never discussed what the service would be like. If we would share, we didn't even know if we could walk that day, but we both felt such a strong presence of God. We didn't want anyone leaving without knowing how very much they are loved, how much God's grace sustains and forgives, and every person in that room could leave knowing they are not without hope... Oh, how He loves us, He loves us.

I do remember being at the front after the service as hundreds came to hug and console us; I wanted to console them as I knew they were also hurting. I didn't want to leave this place that was so full of love and peace. I remember so strongly the funeral director coming to me and saying, you need to leave now and head to the burial; if not, you will be exhausted. The covering I felt from the funeral director and staff was astounding. They moved with patience, compassion, and love. As we exited the church, I looked ahead only to see the hearse with our son's body in it. His body was no longer in his car seat where I could protect him, or in the car with me where we could talk and sing songs together, or in his car and able to wave to him. No, his body wasn't full of life anymore, and my body felt lifeless also as we headed to the gravesite. Drenched in tears and pure exhaustion, I remember being driven in the car staring out the window, wondering to myself, what is next? What will this next painful event hold for me? Will I make it as I see the casket on top of the ground for the last time? I felt the mother lion in me visualize me opening the casket and reaching in to touch in one more time; I knew I couldn't, but that realization that I won't be able to touch him anymore, hug him, feel his hands made me want to literally vomit. The sickening pit in my stomach as we pulled in was way too much at this moment. I don't want to get out of this car and face the bitter cold of the weather and the scene that stood so close to my view. I didn't want to talk to anyone. I wanted to run and escape this. I felt paralyzed with fear of how I would do this.

The song played It Is Well as we stood with family under the tent that covered us and the casket. The brackets that held it above ground would soon be dropped, and he would be covered in dirt. There was a quiet hush, no words just weeping, tears, snot; yes, snot poured out, and not one person cared. It hurt, this day hurt too bad to care, it felt cold, it felt gray, it felt raw, and it wasn't supposed to be; this only happened in movies. It wasn't a movie; it was our life. I knew we couldn't stay under this tent too long, and they knew we requested not to watch the burial process. So, we all quietly walk to a small little house on the property, a cozy white cottage with fireplaces lit inside. We walked into a cottage where love abided with grief, a place where it offered some comfort of home, a place for us to rest again before we left the place where we leave our son.

I want to thank those who were so comforting, as you were also hurting. So, thank you for being there for our family. Words of advice; don't tell someone who has lost that the person "is in a better place". It's not comforting; it's not going to make them one bit happier or make their sorrow ease. We know all of these things, but we want them here. Let us want them to be here; it's normal; dying isn't supposed to feel good. We know they are no longer suffering, but we are suffering for them; we miss them. We know that heaven is beautiful; we know all the good things about them not having to live here on earth. But our grief is because we will miss them because they had so much more ahead for their lives. We want them here; there is no other way around it; don't dismiss someone's sorrow.

Grief is real, we all deal differently, but we all hurt. I have stood amazed at those who lost a child and were able to write and get the book out so quickly. I read them, and they were healing in many ways because I saw they had hope, but I haven't been truly ready to write about this day until now. Even as I sit here at a Starbucks in a corner and hear quiet chatter all around, I ponder and think, would you ever really be ready? At least sitting here, I can probably assure myself I won't have a breakdown, I can keep it contained, and hopefully, write more where I would usually try to escape for a bit.

I knew what was left of daylight was leaving us darkness was creeping in quickly, and I didn't want to leave the cottage, a little home on the hill where we went to gather, and yet my son, I felt, was left alone in a cold box. It was time to head home to the place that was full of reminders that Caleb wasn't there; there were signs everywhere that our lives had changed. Cars lined up on the street, flowers and plants filled every corner of the home, food lined the countertops.

I was so blessed with special people that would come to donate their time to clean my house, organize my kitchen and food, and just my life. In my mind, before this all happened, I had it all together, oh little did I know. I became completely dependent on Jesus and everyone around me. I had to focus on being strong for my kids, my family. I couldn't be worried about laundry and meals; even my dogs were sent away for a week to make sure they weren't neglected. I remember what was important to me going forward was not staying in bed; when I would lay there, it allowed too much time to think, too much fear, too much anger to enter. If I would at least get out of bed, shower, and get ready for the day, I felt I was taking a step forward even if an hour later, I was taking a step back to bed under the covers. The television would be on because the silence was way too strong; actually, the silence was too much noise for my mind. The only thing was, anytime a song or a commercial would come on, I would jump and scream, "TURN IT OFF". Music could only be on when I was prepared for it. I couldn't even take worship music being on at the beginning unless I was able to completely lay flat on the floor in surrender. I couldn't do it, it was too much pain for me to comprehend, and the melody, the words, the memories hit right in the middle of my stomach.

Unfortunately, most of us at this stage in our lives have been to a funeral, a viewing, or someone's life where they have lost a loved one. We've stood in silence in a corner, not knowing how to comfort the grieving friend or family member. We've watched as someone suffered in pain, and we couldn't stand to see them suffer anymore, we've watched someone as they age, and their life ended as peacefully as it could be. We've heard the horrific nightmares on TV of someone losing their child, or we hear of a friend of a friend who has lost. I honestly didn't think this would be me standing in the corner weeping, and no one could console this pain. So now I know, the greatest thing when you are faced with someone's grief is to be there and pray.

The next morning came, and I wondered how the sun could rise and shine when my son wasn't here. It didn't seem fair that people would soon have to go to work, that life was going on, that people were planning their winter breaks. I am left to deal with this for the rest of my life, and they are already going on. Well, my friend, that's life, and at times, it just stinks like rotten garbage. I don't try to make everything beautiful, and life can be brutally unfair. I have asked God numerous times to explain the fairness of life to me; He hasn't responded just to say, "Be still and Know". Well, that is pretty profound, but He didn't bother to give me directions on how to do that. Did I ever mention I am a fixer? And this couldn't be fixed by depositing money in Caleb's account or calling a therapist, booking a vacation. Heck no, nothing would fix this. I didn't want to leave my house, let alone a vacation. There was no fun to be had, and I didn't want to even think of fun without Caleb; he helped bring the laughter, the memories, the noise. So, I am not ready for anything fun, just rest, some sort of peace, and some sort of validation that this would get better. As the days went by, the crowds of people in my home dwindled down, people began to fly back to their home, others had to head back to work and school, and soon I knew Mackenzie would head back to LA to college and life. I wasn't ready for that either; Micah had to go back to school, and soon Matt back to work.

None of us were ready; how could we be? But life had to go one, bills had to be paid, and school was awaiting. I sensed such pain that day as I held Mackenzie on my porch, telling her, "It will all be ok, we will make it, don't worry." I was strong for my family; I truly was, but they knew the questions in my voice that spoke without saying, "But how will we make it?" One tear at a time, one broken piece at a time, one memory at a time, one occasion at a time, we would make it. His redeeming grace and mercy that renewed every morning would be available for us 24/7. That was our promise, our hope, our answer.

There was never a time I wanted to end my life; I just wanted it to be with him, all of us. I wanted us to be a family again here on earth, the tangible kind, the family that meets for dinner, the family that decides where to go on vacation, the family that sits around the living room and we talk and "share our hearts". I wanted that all back. The word death on earth is so very final; it's so real and yet so hard to comprehend. I still so often find myself shaking my head saying out loud, "Is my son really dead?" It still seems unreal almost four years later. There are things in my life, your life that you may always feel just can't be real. It can also be something so good that you ask yourself, "Is this too good to be true?" I hope it's the latter of these. I want us to have to shake ourselves and feel such joy that we can't contain it. We all deserve to have moments that seem unreal because they are so beyond our dreams but remember, they aren't beyond His plans.

I cannot go to the next chapter without thanking everyone, first my family, you all came in and carried us when we couldn't walk, you sang at the funeral when it was hard for you to even speak, you shared a message of hope, you made his casket personal with special touches of who he was, friends from all over you brought meals, flowers, cards and so much more. This chapter has so many in-betweens, so many moments where I couldn't have functioned without your help.

But here we are, a week after Caleb has died, and it was suddenly, unexpected, shockingly unexpected. And that's where this next chapter begins.

Just Once—One Decision and Forever Changed

The last time I saw him was a Monday, February 8th. He was happy with his cousin Macayla, dressed adorably in his hat and new Doc Martins. I watched his grin as he talked to me so confidently that day, that beautiful contagious smile. Wednesday the 10th came too soon. I immediately knew when I heard Caleb died that it wasn't intentional or an overdose, a sickness; I knew it was a deadly mistake.

Oh, my friends, I will be real, honest, I wasn't the naive mom who thought her children were perfect. I knew Caleb had done things that caused much discussion in our home; as a matter of fact, Caleb would tell you what he had done. So, don't worry if there are any conversations going around about things Caleb may or may not have done; I know them. But as a mom, I do know this one thing, at this particular moment that caused him to take his last breath, it was a Just Once.

I will go a little deeper, and the reason I will go deeper is so you can share the message of how this can happen to anyone. This can be "your Just Once". We won't let Caleb's mistake be hidden in a secret closet because we are afraid of how it will make our family look. That's not ministry or putting purpose in our pain, that's the ugly thing called pride, and I don't want it in my life. I know if Caleb were here right now, he would tell you don't do it. He often would tell his brothers and sisters, "Don't make the same mistakes I made." He was an incredible guy. There wasn't anyone who didn't fall in love with Caleb. He was handsome, charming, and to a fault, could live too much in the moment.

It was a Tuesday evening, and he had gone to have a tattoo filled in that was in honor of his uncle Kevin, my brother, who had passed from cancer. It wasn't a new tattoo but was adding to it to fill in things he wasn't able to afford earlier, and he was using his birthday money. He had called us that evening and was on speaker as we all were in my kitchen, his dad, Micah, and I. He continued to tell us he felt really sick while getting the tattoo done and almost fainted. He sounded shaken up, and we prayed for him and said, "Caleb, go to bed and rest; tomorrow is a new day." We always said, "I Love you" before we hung up. I remember Matt and I laying in bed, sharing with each other that he will feel better tomorrow; probably just got weak and sick to his stomach. Caleb didn't handle pain too well. When he didn't feel good or had a sniffle, I was at his bedside with soup and lots of love. He hated pain. He also had a fear of being sick and dying.

Well, we all know the story I wrote previously that the next day he was gone. A few days after his death, I remember being in my room, and his phone rang, and I answered, and I knew this young man's name because of a text I found. While going through his phone, I had found a text that asked for a pain pill, a prescription pain pill. I remember sitting in my bed with Caleb's phone next to me and the voice on the other end I am sure never dreaming I would answer, and this would be the conversation about the pill he had given my son, which killed him. He asked for Caleb in a very upbeat voice. I said, "Caleb is dead, he isn't here anymore, and that what you gave my son; it killed him."

He began to repeat, "No, No, No."

I spoke calmly, but so strong, I remember crying and saying, "I don't want one more person to die because of the pills you are giving out." He hung up, and I am sure he was in shock but couldn't be near as in shock as I was at even having this conversation.

Listen, I am not angry at this person. I have often envisioned myself meeting him face to face and saying, "I forgive you, God forgives you," and taking him in my arms, but he hasn't asked for forgiveness, so he has to live with it, but my heart has forgiven him. We didn't get the autopsy back for months, but the cause of death was there on the death certificate in letters that seemed to be printed in red (although they weren't) were: "Accidental death, laced with Fentanyl."

One package of what was supposed to be Oxycontin was laced, one pill, he took one pill, and died in his sleep. I don't want to imagine he was in pain because that haunts me, but his heart stopped beating. I often wonder if he tried to get us to tell us he was sorry, if he cried out for help and no one heard him, did he beg God please save me and forgive me? I can't go too far into that night in my mind because it sickens me to think he may have called out for me, and I wasn't there. It sickens me to think he tried to save himself and couldn't. I can't go there too often and too deep because the pain is too excruciating for me.

He went to bed happy, according to his roommates, and we were confident he would be ok tomorrow. Caleb was so excited about life and the week ahead; on Thursday, he was working with his dad, he was in college, he was working at church on Sundays. But, he made a big mistake, a deadly one. He trusted someone with his life, with the pain he felt, he wanted a quick fix because he didn't feel good, and now… he's gone.

I told Caleb until I was blue in the face, don't trust other people with medication, don't drink, don't smoke, don't do this or that. It's not worth it, Caleb; many times, I would hear, "Mom, you are so religious, boring, etc.," but most of all, he would always say, "Mom, I won't do anything stupid." I remember so vividly a few weeks before he died standing over me at the kitchen table, his dad sat to the left of me, and he looked at us and said, "Mom and Dad, thank you for not ever partying with me, I know I would get mad at you both and say I wish you would lighten up, but now I am grateful." That day has given me peace when I have asked myself over and over what more could I have done.

It grieves me to say this, but Caleb was the poster child for "It's not worth it". He was the poster child for "Just having fun can kill." The poster child for "Don't take prescriptions from anyone but a doctor." There are so many things our journey should teach others. It can be just one or two drinks that you feel will lighten up the mood and bring you the confidence to handle the crowded room, and soon you find yourself drunk and now in a position of driving, or being attacked, or not knowing your chemical makeup. You don't know that you possibly started drinking yourself into becoming addicted. These look-alike pain pills are being made even on college campuses. They now have the machines to make the pills and package like a real prescription. Crazy how accessible things are that are killing our youth, killing adults, and no consequences. We have to stop this.

Then there is the pain pill that will just take the edge off of you feeling uptight, or just one more pill for the pain from something that can actually be cured with just a plain Tylenol. Now your body craves something stronger because it is immune to the regular pain pill. Or we think the weed that is so easily accessible now is just for this party I am at but soon becomes a craving, and now it's something I have to also do alone at home, but now that is even laced with Fentanyl. Then soon, the weed needs to be stronger, and I need a drink with the weed, and I am not feeling myself today, let me take another Xanax to just get through the day. Tomorrow will be better. Tomorrow doesn't always come like we think it will. I just want to have sex this one time; I know they love me, and it's Just Once. Soon it becomes something we crave outside of marriage, and yet we know that person isn't the one for us or in love with us, but it temporarily fills the void in my life.

Am I judging? Absolutely not. Have I made mistakes? More than I can count. I know though the consequences of these Just Once can become lifetime addictions, mistakes that haunt us, and like Caleb's brought death. Our mistakes are why we are sharing this story. This isn't a fiction book, my friends, this is the real thing, and we want to save lives and show you God's redemption in the midst of heartbreak. It's not a fun thing to read or discuss, but yet we live in a society of addiction, a world full of instant gratification and of craving something to fill the void, the loneliness we feel, the longing to get through life. It happens subtly, and we don't intentionally want to become addicted and dependent on something that can destroy us. None of us want to be dependent on a pill, drink, or something else, but we've allowed ourselves to think we need it, we want to be fixed immediately, we want this ache to stop immediately. We don't want to feel pain at all, so we numb, we seek, we substitute, and a part of us dies inside slowly. Caleb could have waited and made a wise decision, but he didn't like the way he felt that night, and he told us he felt sick, and he trusted someone that didn't intentionally kill him but did by giving him those pills. You see, like the pill that was laced couldn't be detected by just looking at it, so it is deception. You can't see it always on the outside, it may look perfect and exactly what we need, but if we truly start to seek God and ask Him for wisdom, we can look at the one more drink differently, the jar of pain pills with wisdom, the girl or guy on social media for a hook up.

What if we looked at these temptations as another way to kill us, whether literally or spiritually speaking? No matter what, it destroys us. Can we come back and be healed and overcome addiction? Absolutely by the almighty grace of God and programs that have helped thousands, but why even go there? Why destroy time that could have been better spent? So many times, Matt and I have talked to each other and say if only he had called before taking that, we would have said no, just take a Tylenol. You see, he didn't go to bed thinking that it was laced. His roommates said he was happy, hugged them all goodnight with his McDonald's bag. We think, at times, we are invincible; let me tell you we aren't. It doesn't matter if you were raised in a church home, in a wealthy home, a home with both parents, money, or a home with no adult supervision, no Godly home; whatever your circumstances, we all have temptation. We all fail, we all make mistakes and are tempted, but we have a choice.

Our journey is to tell you no matter what, do not do it, do not think you are different than anyone else and can handle it. I can't handle it; I know my body and barely take anything other than a Tylenol. There is so much to our story, but part of our message is don't get in the car with one ounce of alcohol on you; get a driver. Don't smoke weed and think you won't become addicted and that all weed is ok. Don't take a pill that is packaged and looks just like a real prescription. It can happen to you, to your son, your daughter, your family member, friend, or anyone. We all are in this world, and we have to help one another. Addiction can happen to anyone; one pill can kill anyone; one relationship that isn't good can destroy us.

But here we stand after Caleb's death to tell you we aren't without hope; we are alive and living. We never want you or anyone to go through this pain. That is why I am honest with you and vulnerable. It doesn't feel good to tell you Caleb made a stupid decision, but I thought about it so much before writing this book, and that's what Caleb would want me to do. He was an honest child, and he would want you to know that it isn't worth it. It's caused his family and friends pain, and I know if Caleb had stopped to think for a second that this could kill me and cause my family great sorrow, he would have thrown it as far as he could and never tried it.

So here I am, wondering why my child, but I often hear God ask, "Why not Caleb?" He made a poor, poor choice that night on February 9th, that evening he made a decision to fix a temporary pain, not knowing he would leave us here on earth permanently pained. It happened, and it can happen to any of us. It can happen to those who think they are perfect; it can happen to the one who has never taken a sip of alcohol or even taken a puff of a cigarette. Life happens, addictions and habits are formed, and deadly one-time mistakes can take us away. It's called life here on earth. Oh, it's a beautiful world, there is so much beauty in people, in the sky, the land, the sea, but there are also temptations, temporary things we call solutions, and my friends, there is no easy fix to pain. Walk through it, cry through it, pray through it, but just remember, Just Once is our story, and we don't want it to be anyone else's. I don't have any enemies that I know of, but if I did, I wouldn't wish it on my worst enemy. It's too much to repair; it's too painful to wish this on anyone. So as a family, we will warn you from the mountaintops, don't do it, just don't do it.

I want to badly to say four years later, I have seen a decline in these deadly mistakes, but it has actually gone up. More accidental deaths all over the world, and yet it doesn't seem to get the attention it needs for awareness. We think it can't happen to us, it won't happen to us, it's not around me, oh my it's everywhere and very easy to get a hold of.

Addiction, suicide, drugs, alcohol, sex addictions are flooding the lives of people; families from every walk of life are burying their children. It can be a Just Once for many of these people, it can be just a party that seems innocent enough, and a life can be gone. What can we do? Be aware, share our story, share that a few moments of fun or pain relief aren't worth the agony that many will suffer because of it. My heart is to share that you are never without hope, never without a Heavenly Father that will never leave you, nor forsake you.

When I weep sometimes and can't seem to stop, I know He is weeping with me. His heart is so tender towards us, our sorrows and pain, He doesn't become a "dead beat dad," our Father is without flaws, without sin, and yet He loves us in our junk. Just Once isn't worth it. I never ever can say it enough. I love you and your family and don't want you to suffer. So, they may say you "nag" them too much; it's okay because you love them, and if it has to be so embedded in their minds, then so be it. Nag on mom and dad, nag on…

Just One More Time
to Hold You

What do you long for in life? We start off as a child just being so grateful for life, a new toy, a new pair of shoes, the playdate with our friends. Life is so simple when little, or at least it should be.

We enter into our teenage years, and our wants and desires start to be a little mixed with all the changes going on, hormones, and possibly even life situations. We long to just fit in, to have the car that all the other friends seem to have, the date to the prom, the grades to graduate. Our longings become more than they were in elementary school and a little deeper. They seem to become a little harder to obtain than just the Christmas list we wrote for Santa.

Then our twenties, we are supposed to figure out what we are to do with the rest of our lives. We may or may not have graduated from college, or maybe have decided college isn't for me. We look ahead to the future with anticipation and yet so many questions of how will I provide for myself, will this career make me happy, will I ever find the one for me? We seek so many things; the twenties were hard years for me. Of course, not compared to now, but they were tough. I wasn't sure exactly where I was supposed to be at my age, a part of me felt like I was an adult, and another part of me wanted to run home to mom and stay in bed all day and have her make me soup. I got married at twenty-two and loved it, no regrets, but at times, I did still want my mom.

No one understood my emotions as my mom did at that age, and I didn't know if this whole thing of going to work, coming home, cleaning, and cooking was what it felt like when I would "play" house with my little make-believe imagination full of teapots and tiny kitchens. I wanted to be perfect, and I didn't have it all together even to begin to know how to achieve this. Now that I am older, I know that isn't even possible. After many mistakes, I realize perfection isn't attainable here on earth. I just longed to find out what would make me happy all the time. I didn't realize what I really was longing for was something that could only come from Jesus. I needed more than the emotional Sunday service; I needed a 24/7 relationship.

When I became a mom, I do know I felt the closest to what the love of Jesus must feel like, but not anywhere near the love He has for us. Becoming a mom gave me a longing as never before to become a better person, to love more, to spend as much time as I could with my children. I longed to raise them in the way that they would know the center of their world couldn't be mom or dad but Jesus. I longed to be a mom who could have a spotless house, happy children, and a happy husband. My longings weren't probably that different than many of you that read this. I wasn't longing for something that seemed too difficult. I just wanted to be the mom that my kids would honor and respect. I continued to long from my children for something that you truly can only find from what God gives us. We often expect our kids to say the things about us that the Father already speaks over us, we aren't perfect but forgiven, we are loved, we are created in His image.

My longings weren't out of reach. They were all touchable, tangible things. Until…

Until now, until the day everything I was able to do, be, share, touch with Caleb was gone. There is a smell that, as moms, we understand that each child has; even Matt has said so many times, "I miss his smell." I remember from the day he was born the little baby breath smell, the smell of baby lotion on his skin, then the smell as he grew of beach baby with sunscreen smell, the smells of my sweaty boy after playing sports and being outside all day. Then the smell of his clothes. I long for Caleb's scent. I often go hug his jacket in hopes the smell will remain. It has faded but somehow, just breathing in his jacket rekindles those memories. I long for his scent.

I long for his hands, those chubby little hands that once rested in my hands as his security soon grew to long fingers and thin hands. They were masculine but yet beautiful. I saw those hands do many things. I saw them worship; I saw them use his gifts on the piano. I saw them strum his guitar; I saw those hands draw and write in his journal. I would watch his hands so often and think to myself, What will those hands truly be used for that pleases God. A few weeks before he died, he was at home and didn't feel good. I told him to lay with me in my room, he was feverish, and I remember reaching over and grabbing his hand and saying, "Caleb, I love your hands." I silently prayed over those hands, asking God to heal and protect him. I remember it as if it is happening right now; I just couldn't let his hand go. I traced his fingers and remembered just praying; that's all I could do.

I long for his voice, the little boy voice that would say "Mommy," the little raspy voice that would say "I scared," the teenage voice that would holler down and ask "What's for dinner," the little boy voice that sang "Happy Birthday Jesus," then soon grew into this singing voice that would make me stop everything just to sit and listen to him sing. It was a unique, strong, powerful voice with an edge. I would ask him to just please sing and play the piano or guitar. He was pretty much always down to share his talent, and he didn't fight me on it because Caleb knew it was truly a gift that God gave him, and he found passion in using his gifts. He knew I couldn't get enough of it. It motivated him, it inspired him, and it ministered not just to others but to him as well. I think he knew God loved him when he would sing. I felt he was thankful for that talent. I long for his voice to sing loudly with me in the car. I long for his voice to say, "Mom, listen to this song I wrote today." Most of all, I long for "Mom, I love you."

I long for his humor. It started young. Caleb found great joy in humor; from the time he was little, he loved to make us laugh as a little boy does. We would even have him repeat things he would say or do because it would make us laugh so bad. I don't say this pridefully, but Caleb, literally from a small child, would make people happy. He longed to make people smile and laugh. As he grew older, sometimes he knew his humor might have aggravated me a little too much. He may have pushed it a little too hard. Like the time he hid and blew his lifeguard whistle so loud with commands as I came out of my room, or the prank calls he would make. There were so many, and many of these we have on video. He found such joy in laughter, and to be honest, he gets that rightfully from Matt and me. We will laugh until our stomach hurts, and it's usually at each other. The laughter we found as a family, heals. I long for a belly laugh with Caleb, a roll on the floor and laugh. Maybe I wouldn't even get upset if it wasn't completely appropriate— lighten up, you wouldn't either.

I long for your hugs. We have always been a very affectionate family. I kind of get a little awkward when I realize someone else isn't a hugger. We are a hugging family, a kiss on the cheek family, a squeeze you until it hurts kind of love. As a child, he never ceased to amaze us with his affection, from hugs, kisses to outward vocal expressions no matter who was around of "I love you to everyone that was around him."

I think if you ask anyone who knew him well, they will tell you the same. Caleb loved to give affection and get affection. As soon as he would enter the front door of our home after putting down his guitar case, he would come hug everyone. I long for his hug. I would stand on my tiptoes, and he would bed down, and we would hug. I know if he came back and hugged me now, I wouldn't let go; it wouldn't be possible. I would be too afraid he would leave.

I long for conversations. Caleb learned to communicate from a very young age, and at times, I had to remind myself how young he was. He was also very inquisitive, lots and lots of questions. As he grew older, I realize there were times I didn't have the answers; actually, many times, I didn't know the answers. As he grew older, our conversations were full of laughter, and we, as most parents could say, had our disagreements or discussions that were deeper than my own understanding, and I would answer with, "Caleb, I don't know the answer, but God does." He questioned why bad things happened to wonderful people. He didn't understand why we suffered pain. He watched his uncle and grandad within a few years of each other suffer from cancer and die. It hurt him as he believed with us for their healing, and it didn't come the way we prayed. Yet, he saw the faithfulness of God in our suffering and his pain. I would love to sit with him and hear him tell me how now his questions are all answered and how it's way more wonderful than we spoke and read about. I long just to hear his voice. I wouldn't fret about not knowing the answers now; I would just listen and reassure him that God is so aware. I wouldn't search and dig, google, and ask to find answers. I simply would just listen and trust in the knowing God knows.

I long for a dream of my boy. It has been my greatest longing since I know his physical body is gone. It is a desire I have prayed and asked God for. Can you believe he hasn't come to me once in a dream? I want him to come speak to me, tell me something. Tell me, "Mom, I am sorry," he loves me, and how wonderful heaven is. I would love to dream; many tell me it's because I am not ready yet and that it may be too painful, and a part of me knows that is true, but I am ready. Or will I ever be ready? I know if I could just see him in my dreams, it would break my heart when I awaken, or would it maybe bring me security in knowing he is happy.

I long for it all, I long, oh how I long for Just Once, give me just one more moment with him. One more smell of his skin, one more touch of his hand, one more hug, one more sound from his voice, one more belly laugh, one more conversation about Jesus. Just Once…

Just Once—One Touch from Jesus

This may sound so simple, and I don't try to make it sound that way because pain isn't simple. Pain is complex, deep, and depending on the hurt, it can be a pain that is forever here on earth or something that takes years and counseling to overcome. But yet, when people ask me how I have made it this far without giving up, I will tell you over and over again the reason, and the definite reason is Jesus. Jesus Christ, my Savior, has helped me to face this unbearable pain.

Many may ask if He is such a good God, then why didn't He save Caleb? Why have you suffered such loss from a God you say is good? Well, I don't have all the answers, but I know this one thing He never promised us that we wouldn't suffer while on this earth; He promised He wouldn't leave us nor forsake us, and He hasn't.

Have we at times felt it was too much to overcome, to face, to forgive? Oh, indeed, we have. There isn't a protein or energy drink on this earth that could give us the strength to sustain this pain as He has. My biggest prayer has been, God, let my life be a testimony of your faithfulness so that others may know how truly good you are to me. I want others to see a reflection of you in me, I want others to know I personally continue to fail and doubt, but you haven't changed.

There have been nights and days that I didn't feel like going on, I felt like giving up, I felt angry, I felt such deep sorrow I couldn't talk to God. Then I would find myself realizing I am incapable of living without Him. "I need Thee, Oh I need Thee, Every Hour I need Thee." I live it out because there isn't an hour that goes by that I don't need Jesus. I am not so heavenly bound that I am no earthly good. I am as human as anyone else, but for me personally, I don't have the strength on my own to do life period, before or after Caleb's death.

My prayer has been for a true revival to spread over the communities, counties, cities, states, and worldwide. I ache for others, I see what others are facing, and I hurt for them and even greater if they feel they have no hope. I want to introduce them to the one who saved me when all hope was gone. I want them to meet the one who held us up when our physical bodies had collapsed on the floor. I want them to hear the voice of God, who said, "My grace is made sufficient for you" (2 Corinthians 12:9 NIV). I want them to know they, too, can have laughter again. They, too, can take the pain they are suffering and find strength and then spread hope to someone else. I want the world to know there is a place they can go to, fall on their knees in surrender, and have God invade every corner of their life. I want to share with you this Father, this healer, this comforter. I want you to have this experience that brings light in the darkness, which pours down an oil from heaven to heal and comfort. It is Just Once saying, "God, I need thee," Just Once, "Father forgive me," and I promise you this, Just Once that touch from Him and we are given new mercies, our sins are forgiven, and hope is restored.

We want an instant fix; of course, we do. Why wouldn't we? It's a natural thing to want to have pain immediately alleviated from our lives. I just wish it could be that way, but yet this pain has made me grow into someone I would never have. I can honestly say, I would have probably been a little prideful if my life would have been perfect, God allowed things in my life from a young age, and it squandered all I thought that was perfect about my life.

Yes, I said, "God allowed" did God want Caleb to swallow a pill and die? Absolutely not, but we truly are given a free will. Could God, who healed the blind and raised the dead, have stopped this fatal death? Yes… He could have.

In all honesty, many of us have questioned why God allowed it. This wasn't something God wanted for Caleb, but we make decisions. Most decisions we make on a daily basis aren't life and death decisions. They are just decisions about what to eat, what to wear, should I exercise? Not should I take this pill today and trust someone who gave it to me.

I don't blame God. I actually don't blame anyone, not even Caleb. Although Caleb made a foolish choice and didn't put much thought into the consequences, I don't blame him. It was a life mistake, a mistake that has cost us all such great pain, yes God could have stopped it, but He didn't, and so I will trust that God is trusting us with this pain. He has trusted us to carry this sorrow, and that I know, and I will be secure in it. I have often imagined the story that the world would hear if Caleb would have been brought back to life, and he was telling us how beautiful heaven was, but his time on earth wasn't over, and it was to spread the word of Just Once. I often imagine him coming back and telling us how sorry he was, telling us what it felt like when he entered into this new realm with Jesus. I imagine so many things about what would have transpired had God spared him his life. Yet, we know not of the reasons. I don't understand young children dying of cancer, diseases, abuse, on and on. I have heard many times, why would I want to serve this God you speak so highly of when all I see is pain around me? The world doesn't look too good right now, wars, suicide, addiction, anger, poverty, and yet I would still say, "but He is still good." The truth is we can't hide from it. We are in the world, and life will bring suffering and heartache. Our promise is that He hears our groans, He feels our anger. He hasn't decided to step aside and get back to us later; He doesn't abandon us. No matter how alone you feel… you never are.

I feel we need to get out of questioning so much with God and just literally surrender, and I haven't conquered that yet. I don't understand everything, many things actually, but yet, I won't understand anything clearly until I am with Him in eternity.

I realize, for now, it feels good just to trust. It feels good to just rest in it. Let's admit, we have all had trust broken somewhere, at some point in our walk. Unfortunately, it happens at all too young of an age, and sometimes those trust issues can linger and cause a lot of dysfunctional actions on our part. It's hard to retrain a mind that has been hurt over and over again and believe that God is still so good. I get it, I really do.

I can't relate to someone who has been physically and emotionally abused. That's not my place of expertise that I can go to and say, "I know how you feel," but I can pray for you, with you and listen. We can all agree trust can be broken in many ways, maybe some boyfriends in high school that broke up with you, and you felt you would never love again (and yes, I think we all have that one breakup). You thought he was the one that would father your children, and then buy your first home together, establish a future. Then you grow up, and you get hurt, and disappointments come, then another hurt comes before you are even healed from the first one, and you realize this isn't fun. You begin to sense a wall being built up. You look at life always with a question. If something feels happy, you begin to think something bad will happen soon. You find yourself becoming bitter, making excuses for your behavior, anger builds up, hopelessness starts to invade, and you find there is no one you can trust. Brokenness seems to be your story, chapter after chapter of heartbreak. You feel life has dealt you a bad hand, you feel abandoned, fearful and our hearts become so guarded, and walls begin to be built to protect ourselves.

Looking back to when my dad left, I know that I put up a little wall that would protect my mom. Any man that seemed to enter our world, I looked at with apprehension. Will you leave us also? Will you hurt my mom? Yet, I also remember the life my mom continued to live out in front of us. It wasn't one of being the victim. She was always finding the good in things and always giving thanks to God. Sometimes, I wanted to say, "Mom, get real life is really sucking right now." Yet, when she was discouraged, and she was human, and I would see her cry, but soon after, she would be in her room, praying loudly to God. It taught me something at a young age; my mom couldn't fix our pain by getting remarried, she couldn't teach us to trust again by taking us to special courses designed for children of divorced parents; she taught it by living it out.

I was blessed, and I don't take it for granted. Many of you have lost your mothers, and I ache for you because they truly are your best friends as you age. I don't take it for granted, and again, that's a sorrow I can't relate to. I know the loss of my dad was hard; my brother and now Caleb are unbearable at times, but I have my mom, and for that, I am so grateful. I write all this to say, trust gets broken, people fail, we make dumb decisions at times, and heartbreak of some kind is inevitable. I can't promise you anything in life. I wish this book could give you all the correct answers on how to raise a child, a teenager, how to deal perfectly with heartache. I don't have the answers. I often have struggled with the thoughts probably made up in my head of people saying, "Why would I want advice from her? She lost her son, she failed?" I know that's not good thinking, but I told you I don't lie. But then I think that's exactly why you should listen to me. Learn from my mistakes, learn from my honesty, learn from Caleb's decision. But most importantly, know that I live and speak the truth, and that is, He is a God who "will never leave you, nor forsake you" (Hebrews 13:5 NKJV).

Be strong and courageous. Do not be afraid or terrified because of them, for the LORD your God goes with you; he will never leave you nor forsake you.

—Deuteronomy 13:6 NIV

RHONDA LUCAS

I'll Be Home for Christmas

Christmas, the magical season… As a child, I remember getting the Sears and JC Penny Catalog and looking through it and drawing circles around the things I wanted. For some reason, I thought maybe I would get the 100 things I circled. The smells of the fresh cut tree in our house and homemade cookies we would cut out with the cookie cutters and the homemade icing that dripped over the cookies—I remember how we would have our tiny fingers covered in it and licking it off. Then a cup of milk to end the night with fresh cookies to dip in it. Oh, I loved those days.

There was the magic of hearing the noise of gift wrapping and trying to guess what my mom and dad were wrapping and then what in the world Santa would bring down the chimney. I never understood how he would come down that chimney while a fire was burning fiercely, but I didn't doubt for too long because I liked believing in someone that brought so much joy to everyone. Doubting wasn't something I was known to do as a child, I just believed and if someone said it, I trusted it. I wanted to believe in something that didn't seem possible. I wanted to believe that there was this overweight adorable, happy, cheerful, white-bearded man that was in love with life and children and wanted to make them happy. After all, it's what Jesus wants us to be, happy and givers, and Santa fit this job perfectly. Christmas was the time of year that I dreamed big. I couldn't wait to see my little sisters face on Christmas morning and her playing with all her toys; for some reason, that was one of my favorite parts. I loved my mom and dad waking us up early to come and see what Santa brought.

But then life changed for our family when my parents suddenly got a divorce. The magic seemed to leave the home not just at Christmas but all the time. I was no longer the blessed child of a two-parent home. I wasn't getting off the bus anymore to my mom greeting me.

I was the product of a now single-parent home, a mom that had to go to work, and a brother that quit high school early to help provide for my mom. Santa Claus couldn't fix this, not on Christmas or any day. My life had been forever changed, and my trust was broken. I began to doubt if the feeling of Christmas would ever return. But isn't that what happens to us? We will find our lives so quickly turned upside down and wonder how in the world we will ever be happy again, how will anything ever feel like it did before? If we are honest, it usually doesn't go back to the way it was before because we have matured during this change and see things differently. We realize life isn't able to be fixed by taking a trip to Disney World. Life changes us, and the innocence we had before we were affected by the disappointments from people we love and the consequences of mistakes. I had to grow up quickly when my parents divorced. I had to become a little mom when my mom wasn't around and had to work. I felt myself worrying about money, food, and how we would ever have a Christmas again.

The first year my dad was gone was not a happy one. We all tried, my mom tried, but the tears fell down her cheeks, the longing for what was and the magic she once felt was gone. I remember opening the baby doll that was on my Christmas list that I wanted, and it didn't seem quite as exciting as when my dad was there to watch me open it. And yet more than myself, I remember wanting to make everyone happy. I was too young for this to become my mission, but it did. Quietly I would question God and ask, "Why us?"

It got easier as the years went by, and we found our own new happiness. I remember one of my best Christmases was when I was in high school, and I worked during Christmas for a friend of my moms who had a mortgage business. I got my paycheck, and I felt rich. I couldn't wait to go shopping for my family. I will never forget I got my mom a pair of KEDS; they were clean, white, and brand new, exactly what she deserved. I couldn't wait for her to open them. It meant so much to me to be able to buy her something I worked for. I felt magic in giving. I truly knew how Santa must have felt.

As I grew up and the years went by, becoming a parent was what true magic was about and especially at Christmas. When you have children, Christmas takes on a whole new meaning. Yes, Jesus is the center, and we love the little ones playing the role of Mary and Joseph, the plays at school where they all are singing so loud and all the parents beaming with pride. The season where runny noses are a normal and you just pray, they can make it through the end of the year at school so they can attend the Christmas parties where even more germs are exchanged. Having our first Christmas with Caleb was magical, and I remember feeling my heart had a new sense of hope. This was going to be my life, and it was perfect. Mackenzie and Micah only added to the chaos of Christmas, making it even more perfect. Three different piles of presents under the tree, three pairs of pajamas the night before that they would wear to bed full of excitement. Two cookies and milk were left on the counter on the perfect Christmas plate that was just for Santa Claus. The sweetness that filled the home was seriously like honey, nothing but love and blessings. It was Christmas, and we were a family, and this was my dream in life, and I am living it out. What did I do to deserve such happiness? This wasn't just one Christmas; this was years and years I was blessed with memories of my children, husband, and family. If only to go back … Just Once

Fast forward many years, and now the song seemed to play loudly in my mind, and the words "you can count on me… if only in my dreams." The song I'll be Home for Christmas played long before the season had even started. I knew what was approaching, yet time couldn't prepare me.

The first of many to come, our first Christmas without Caleb, and now as I write, I am approaching the second year, yet the hurt and melody of the song plays louder and louder in my heart. The melody and the harmony seemed to echo over and over as I begged it to stop. Please stop, God have mercy on me. As the years go by, it will be replayed over and over. You see, it's real now; this will forever be my Christmas.

In this chapter, you will notice I go back to my childhood and then where we are now in our lives. It's because they are so intertwined together. I see so much of my childhood, and those feelings come so strongly back now as I celebrate a new kind of season.

When I was a little girl at Christmas, I never asked for too much, or should I say, nothing expensive, but yet I would count my presents that were under the tree. I would slowly unwrap and then linger on and watch my brother and sister open theirs. I wanted to prolong the "opening of the last gift". The last gift meant I wouldn't really have presents this awesome for another year. As a young girl raised by my single mom, I knew she wasn't writing Santa asking him for gifts but on her knees asking God to provide food for the table.

No matter what our circumstances were, the Christmas season in our home was full of hope, magical times, and for a moment, a little bit of a fairytale. I could feel the excitement weeks before starting in me. It began as soon as Thanksgiving approached. We would simmer pot-pourri, and the house would smell like everything Christmas should be, Christmas pies and sugar cookies.

It was a time for me to pretend, a time when youth is evident because although we knew things aren't perfect, that baby doll and boxes of wrapped gifts sitting under the tree take us off to our little world of pretend. Don't we have those memories, and sometimes, we can still pretend, for a moment, a second, things are perfect and innocent, and life is all good?

Oh, my oh my, there are things you can't avoid as you grow up. I can't avoid the songs playing loudly at the store, the family photos arriving in my mailbox, the family events where we no longer hear Caleb's voice loudly in the room.

It can be a silent moan, a silent scream, a silent cry, and yet we move, we walk, we awaken, I wrap gifts, I bake cookies, I decorate. My senses haven't left, probably a little stronger, I smell the fragrance of a fresh-cut tree, I live and function, I do, but oh so differently.

You see, when we experience tragedy, we have a choice, many choices. How will you handle your suffering when I'll be Home for Christmas is playing in the background, the pounding of the heart and gut-wrenching, longing for what was consumes you for a moment? How will I handle the presents on Christmas morning that don't have

Caleb's name on them? How?

The first Christmas Eve, we felt changing the normal routine would help to ease the pain. This didn't come with lots of energy, but with a lot of mental work. We pushed ourselves, we dressed up, went to the Christmas Eve service, held the candle up, but barely the strength to do so. We tried hard to make a new normal because that's what you have to do. Normally dinner and Christmas Eve would be celebrated at our home with lots of food, family, and noise. This year was the first of many to come, and we went to dinner at a lovely restaurant where there were small planes that flew in and out as we ate dinner, and the runway was lit up beautifully. I remember sitting at the table looking out the window, and I felt the tears coming. I wiped them quickly so no one would see, but it was clear, sorrow was at our table, the empty chair, the tears fell, and I gave in. I let them fall. Grief couldn't be contained at that moment, and I didn't care.

The families that gathered at other tables seemed so happy and perfect to me were a blurred picture because as I watched them as the tears continued. Why Me? Why my family? Why? Why?

Caleb wasn't coming home from college with his car loaded up with dirty laundry; he wasn't coming home from war or a vacation with friends. There wouldn't be a positive outlook in our thoughts for the promise of next year that he would be home, only the devastating reality that Caleb was gone.

This Christmas, year two was different. You would think I would know what to do, what to expect, yet I didn't. Certain things are easier, and that would be this, I no longer fight the tears when they come. They come I let them fall wherever I am, and I don't care who sees. I don't care if mascara is all over my face (Just for a little while). I realize most of the time, my face is swollen from tears and lack of sleep. I call the bags under my eyes "pockets for tears". There are certain things I don't think a plastic surgeon could fix on me. A plastic surgeon can pull my face tighter, lift my eyebrows, but he can't fix the hole in my heart. The ache that I have grown accustomed to in my body won't heal; only Jesus can provide the grace and strength and the promises of the day that I will be healed and whole.

What in your life is so painful that even the brightest Christmas lights can't fix, what longing is so strong that even a room full of family and friends can't fill the void? The presents wrapped with the biggest bow can't comfort you when the fears, sorrow, and ache fill every fiber of your being.

No, Caleb won't be home for Christmas, but yet I awoke on my second Christmas, and he wasn't waiting on the fireplace ledge like he used to be. I didn't receive a text from him asking if they can come down from upstairs yet at 5 a.m. But we made it, we had hope, we unwrapped gifts, and I think we savored the moments more because now we live for the moments that have joy. I watched my Mackenzie and Micah unwrap the gifts that were on their list with smiles and "Thank you, Mom and Dad."

What did your Christmas list look like this year or last year? What are the real presents of the heart that you opened or maybe didn't receive? What was the longing for this season to bring you and your family? What was it that would have made your heart feel better?

We, as humans, find magical moments in the Christmas season. No matter what we are going through, we still believe that the Savior who was a miracle for all of mankind is so aware of us, and this season is a season of miracles; the grief is ever-present, but the miracle of hope is alive.

Crazy enough, I often believe I can see Caleb opening his gifts, making breakfast. I see it not because of the "spooky magic," but I would call it the Majestic Master.

Because a baby was born in a stable, not Pottery Barn or a Restoration Hardware building, but wrapped in whatever cloths they had. Because of that birth, we can have hope; we can believe in the magic of humanity, kindness, and compassion. That was the greatest Christmas ever… the day the Messiah came to this earth to be born into a world of sin and yet was chosen to bring hope, grace, and peace to a world where death can loom, anxiety, and fear can hover us. But HE was born, and now we must live.

Is There Lipstick on My Teeth?

Let's be honest with one another. Let's just get real here. If you are over forty, you probably can relate more to this chapter than the young ones reading this. If you are young, please read this and appreciate your youth even more.

I will never forget when I read an article Oprah wrote, and it was about aging. She was saying that the fifties were going to be the best; you finally come into yourself and know who you are and what you want.

I, at the time, probably didn't appreciate it because I wasn't quite there yet, but I never forgot it. I didn't forget it because my thirties were awesome. I loved absolutely loved being in my thirties. I felt, at that time, I knew who I was. My purpose was being fulfilled. I was thriving, I felt, at being a mom; I had my last baby boy Micah Seth at thirty-two and was able to go back to my pre-pregnancy body pretty quickly. We were moving into our newly built home in 2001; the kids were still pretty easy, we were busy but loving life. Vacations were a breeze. The kids weren't old enough to argue over where they wanted to go and still not old enough to bring friends. All was well.

Not perfect, there were days, of course, I would look in the mirror and start to notice a few little wrinkles here and there. It was the age of comparing, the age your kids are growing a little more, and you start to notice what they are naturally gifted in or not gifted in. Being in my thirties felt good, felt right, and my biggest fear, at times, was if I had lipstick on my teeth.

Forties came with not so much of a bang as far as celebrations, but it wasn't dreaded. Matt and I had a nice getaway to a beautiful place in Florida that I thought for sure we would one day own. We are working on that, but college, car repairs, and weddings kind of overshadowed that for a while. Things were changing. I was getting a little sad that I would eat pizza, and I felt it was lingering a little longer. It didn't seem to bother me too much. I would enjoy the simple things when I could, then cut back and lose those extra pounds. It was so much easier to lose than it is now. Then death invaded our lives, and the forties just weren't fun. I was forty-nine when Caleb died.

Lipstick on the teeth? I was lucky if that was my biggest issue. I just wanted to make sure I could find some lipstick to put on my lips to override the swollen eyes and tear-stained face. Can I just go back to my thirties? The thirties were the age for me where sometimes the hardest part of our week was finding a time to be alone with my husband without kids banging on the door and my daughter Mackenzie putting notes under the door as if she was abandoned. At the time, those issues seemed to be hard.

Yes, we would have days of tears, flu, disappointments of not winning the baseball game, getting the raise we felt Matt deserved. That was life. I just wanted to run back to those days and simply just have lipstick on my teeth.

How many of you women have ever been out a whole evening with your husband in a group of others, and it's not until you get in the car on the way home, look in the mirror and realize you do have lipstick on your teeth or a nice piece of something green in your teeth? They didn't notice, always seems to be Matts response, "I didn't see it." You were with me all night, and you didn't seem to notice what others are now probably discussing in their car about me? Now at my age, I would probably be a little agitated but may laugh it off as well, "such is life."

Aging, experiences, life, both good and bad, teach us so much about who we are and what matters. I find laughing at the things I can, has helped our marriage and our pain so much. Matt and I both love clothes; we will be the first to tell you that. I will also tell you that many times, we have felt confident about our cute new outfit only to find out when we get home, the tags were hanging off. Why in the world would we be out with such eagerness to wear it then not think to look for the tags? Even worse is when it's the strip of your size going down your leg, usually on jeans. Well, that's great now the world knows what size I am. I told you being prideful doesn't last long for Matt or myself. Actually, I am glad about it. God hasn't let us get away with thinking we are better, we are more worthy, we have it all together. The reason I believe He has allowed us to be humbled many a times is to teach us to be totally dependent on Him.

Aging can be funny if you think about it; we can Botox it up, lift it up, and all too many times suppress it with Spanx. Those things are painful. I am the woman who barely wears them, and then in the pictures, it shows, wow, she needed those Spanx, yet I feel so claustrophobic I seriously get breathing issues. Go ahead, laugh, and picture me either not breathing well or just enjoying life a little too much.

What are we going to do with the mixture of sorrow and joy? How can it all happen at once? Oil and vinegar don't mix; that's proven, yet when on a salad, it tastes so good. Sorrow can be our circumstances that happen without warning, pain that we can't help but have joy is what comes in knowing that though our circumstances haven't changed, and our hearts still ache, but we can trust in the joy that only comes from knowing He is with us. Remember, He doesn't forsake us in the good or the bad times. At the funeral, I didn't feel happy not once, but yet I had an inner hope that we would be okay, that somewhere JOY was going to appear. No, Caleb wouldn't be back, but we could still trust that one day we will see him again, and we will laugh again at times, and most of all, our joy won't come from our circumstances but in the promise of Him.

I don't know where you are in the aging process, maybe you look and feel better than ever, and that's my prayer. If you do, be grateful and enjoy it. To be honest, I don't feel too bad about myself. I think it's because I am not making it my biggest issue. I love taking care of myself the best I can. I love shopping, getting nails done, laying in the sun (don't judge), I love to walk, and a lot of other good things. Sometimes though, life just can give you seasons where you feel you have aged ten years in a month. Then you feel life back in you and some youth restored. Then you go through seasons of just life being blah, the months of January and February where we long for some sun to peek through the clouds.

Sometimes there are so many things that can wear us down. Just the mundane of life, financial pressures, hormones (those lovely things are even greater as you age, said no one ever), and we can find ourselves in a rut. A place where we don't know how we got there, but we aren't moving, and it can become depressing. It's those times we have to push and push harder.

I am writing this as I am living through it at this moment. I am fifty-two; my hormones are crazy. I thought I had gone through the change of life only to have the doctor and cycles of life tell me, oh no, you aren't done yet. Talk about raging hormones. God, can you please make something easy for me? I have literally prayed this. I have researched, studied hormones, vitamins, etc. I have read things I can do to get through this the easiest and fastest way possible. And yet it's still here, and sometimes I feel thirty years old again, and other days I feel I may need a walker. Just kidding, but let's be real; being a woman isn't always easy; then life happens, and we have disappointments and heaviness of life that we sometimes carry even in our posture.

I do know one thing we are incredible creations that only God could make and understand. May each of you, today, find some laughter even if the sun isn't shining; may you find something to do just for you. Take a look in the mirror and if you have something in your teeth, just laugh. If you see an extra wrinkle know my friend, you've earned that. It shows you've experienced life, the joys and sorrows of this rich, beautiful life. You've experienced the highs and lows, your heart has been broken, and you are still here. You are beautiful. You can offer something that's unique to just you. I don't care what you feel your past has done to you; His mercies are new every morning. Even when I awake with the imprints of the pillowcase on my face that have created another wrinkle, I feel Him smiling, saying, "Good morning, beautiful." You are awakened today for a purpose. It may seem unimportant to the world, but it's important to Him.

Go show the world your pearly whites with confidence, and when and if you ever smile and something is in your teeth, just remember no one really cares; they won't lose sleep over it, but just warn your other half to check your teeth, please.

I WILL

I won't lose sleep over one more wrinkle; the day will continue to go on.

I won't find joy in worrying over the past and all that could go wrong.

I won't find hope in looking back over what I thought would be.

I won't find beauty in a world that's full of all of me.

I will find rest in knowing where my source of strength comes from.

I will find darkness cannot stay when we know who formed the sun.

I will find joy as never before, even when nothing has seemed to change.

For I have found He's been greater than anything that I will ever face.

It's Just Another New Year's Eve

I think we all have heard the song It's Just Another New Year's Eve, another night like all the rest, it's just another New Year's Eve, let's make it the best."

Well, here I am on New Year's Eve (NYE), entering into 2020 and going on the fourth year without Caleb. I won't lie; the past few days, I have felt the anguish all over again. We all kind of get the "after Christmas blahs," but I have dreaded it because January and February are such painful landmarks and reminders in my life. I wasn't anticipating this would be my new year's landmarks, not the happy kind throw confetti kind, I mean the painful kind. While many are setting goals of losing weight, cleaning out clutter, better eating and spending habits, I am setting realistic goals of "we can do this" something good is going to happen in the midst of these reminders.

I will be honest; NYE has never been a big deal to me. I always felt it was the great expectation of a complete meltdown and let down. Is it at 12 a.m. that all of our hurts, our baggage, our addictions, fears, and questions go out the door? No, half the time, the world is covering it up with alcohol trying to find joy in that brief moment between 11:59 and 12:00 a.m. We awaken with the same thing we awoke with the day before. Please try to remember I will end this with a positive note. What I am saying is each morning, His mercies are new; each and every morning, His faithfulness is renewed. I can't wait another year for change; I need it now. I need to know I awaken with hope that no matter what I am facing, no matter what you are facing, He is there. He is not a calendar God that only shows up at special events. Oh, how my heart knows this is true. He is there in the midnight hours when the reality jolts you out of a deep sleep in the middle of the night. He is there when you don't know where you will get the money to pay your mortgage. He is there when you are given a diagnosis of a sickness. He is there when you have to choose what casket to bury your child in… He is there.

Yes, it is another New Year's Eve, and we should make it the best, but I want to be real, and for you, my friend, to know He is always there. I am ready for a new season, a season of hope that is greater than my fears, anxiety, my disappointments. I long for a place in my life that is so full of hope that it will sustain me so much in the moments that take my breath away. I don't want to grieve; a mom who has lost doesn't want to feel this pain; we don't crave and long for attention; we long for mercy, for strength, for hope in the darkest of hours.

My goals are truly reset every day because I realize the reality of life happens, and I need to be "real." So this year, this is not a goal list; no there won't be any dynamic outward changes, except I do pray you see Jesus in me more than ever. I pray I will be a reflection of His goodness and the strength that can't be obtained anywhere but through Him. Yes, celebrate this day, make it the best that you can, but know that your best is yet to come. Most drastic changes take time. It's a pulling and tugging of the heart. It's a change that comes through the pains of life and the compassion that comes by walking through things that have softened your heart. We wish we could wave a magic wand, and life would be the glitter we all see on this magical night, but we live in a broken world. A place where people are all searching, and yet we don't have to wait for the ball to drop; He is in each second. It's in the air you breathe, the rising and setting of the sun. I don't speak of things I know nothing of. I speak because I have lived and continue to live this out.

We have a generation seeking for approval, for something to give them a purpose, and it's our job to share the message that we do have hope, purpose, and a life full of beautiful promises, and yet God is the only true source of happiness. Sorrow happens to the rich, poor, famous, the homeless; as long as we live on earth, we each will face sorrow. And yet, in that we still have hope, we can make it, we can enter a new year knowing that He is the same God today as yesterday, that He

RHONDA LUCAS

hadn't left me when the end of December came.

So, I will enter 2020 with a new vision (get it) and a knowing that He that has been faithful will continue to be. I will laugh and have joy, and in the not so happy times, I can promise He will be right there with me and for you, my friend. You can count on that more than anything.

Whether you are dressing up tonight or hanging around in sweats, going to a party or church, or just snuggled up in bed, remember His mercies are new every morning. Happy New Year, Happy New Day…

When a New Year Begins in the Middle of the Week

I thought about what I would name this chapter, my previous one about New Year's Eve was short, but I think you got the message I was trying to share with you.

Now it's the morning of the first. I am tired, but my night wasn't one of late hours and balloons; instead, my eyes were closed a little before midnight, and the soft whispers of I love you and Happy New Year were enough for me. We do have another added benefit when you live in our neighborhood; you feel you are at the best fireworks display that you would have to pay for and drive to, and the noise and booms will remind you it is midnight, so it was a good night. A night of hope, as every night should be, but there are nights we all feel hopeless, nights where we don't feel God in any of our circumstances. How could a God that loves me so much allow the darkness to invade even when it is morning, the sun is out, yet I feel no light? Have you ever just felt that if you can just sleep, you will awaken, and it will all be different? Don't you wish that were true?

I remember when we were in the beginning of our grief with Caleb, we would awaken in the night always around 2–3 a.m. and moan, cry, toss, and turn. We longed for the sun to rise even if we slept during the day; the daylight brought us the realization that we made it through another night. It gave us hope, and that is what God's mercy and grace does. Sometimes, it's just enough, and I mean just enough, but it comes, and we move another step closer to another need for His grace. It is a constant thing. I think when life is really good, and all are blooming in every area of our life, we forget His grace is still there. It's there protecting us from something. It is there allowing us to breathe new life and hope. It is there, so aware of what could have been and what could be. I say I breathe in and out His grace, like oxygen. I need them both to live.

But what do we say about the middle of the week? It is a time where we are halfway through the "work week" or halfway through our time for "payday" almost to another weekend to be with family and friends, and almost "Sunday". We don't feel quite as tired as we did on Monday because we are now anticipating the weekend. I think that is the human nature in us. It's a good day, but not the greatest because we are right in the middle of something in our lives, just waiting for God to get us through till the real breakthrough.

We are longing for the vacation away from our problems, our issues, our mundane routines of life, and yet we are stuck in the middle, the middle of the breakthrough. We see it coming. We feel anticipation mixed with anxiety of "what if it doesn't," yet we know Friday always comes, but how long will it be? How long will I be stuck in this place of waiting for my miracle, my pain to end, my life to be like the friends with the white picket fence and a nice car? How long will it be before my child isn't bullied at school anymore, before our marriage is restored? Are these some of the things you are longing and praying for? And yet stuck, no answers, no major decisions, no smiling face coming out of the school saying, "Mom, I had a good day."—NOTHING HAS CHANGED, and we want out. We want answers.

I promise you this… The anticipation is truly hard; the waiting is like being in a birthing room with no epidural and yet no progress. Just pain, in the end, you know it will be so worth it, but right now, you want to just die. You want to scream, why did I want to have a baby? This hurts too much. We feel this way so very often because we know there is something so much better. God has intended for our life to be full of His goodness, full of the beauty in the world, and yet… we sit and wait, we question, we doubt.

One of the greatest things I heard after Caleb died was that God could handle my questions. I felt those words come to my level and felt, wow, He is hurting with me, He is weeping with me, and He is in the waiting with me. Oh, how our Jesus waits with us, but He also sees

RHONDA LUCAS

the growth that needs to take place in the waiting, the beautiful birth that will take place when we are fully prepared.

I wish I could tell you when, how, and what will happen for you, I don't know for myself. I just want to be faithful in the waiting. I want to find more of Him, so I can become less of me. I looked up the definition of the word "middle" this struck me in the core of my being, or should I say the "middle". "The position of being among or in the midst of something in the middle of the crowd, something intermediate between extreme."

We know we aren't where we started in this journey where the pain began, but oh how my patience can wear out just feeling stagnant in the pain. Do you ever want to go to a room and scream and then just come out, and all the anger, the fear, and the anguish would just be gone? I have heard and seen on television about these places that are called "scream rooms" and used for just that purpose. Can you imagine just truly being rid of all the pain we have? Well, I can't promise you a scream will do that, but I can promise you this, He is in the midst, and oh how He loves us. I know I have said it before, but I feel closest to Him when I am hurting; why? Well, as moms, when our kids are hurting, we just want to "fix it". We will sleep with them; we will coddle, maybe even spoil a little bit, pray, and love on them so much. Why? Because when they hurt, we hurt. So, I know when we are hurting, our Heavenly Father is hurting with us and even more for us than we do for ourselves. Imagine a perfect parent; He is that.

Sometimes the truth is, we just have to wait. We just have to wait. Did I say "wait"? I am sick of waiting to be healed, sick and tired of grief, loss, and sorrow. The truth is, I won't be completely healed from my loss until I am with Caleb again for eternity.

What do I do in the waiting? I have to be completely dependent on God. When I have a breakthrough of any kind, I do not, I repeat, I do not take it for granted. When joy comes, I enter it fully. I don't suffocate it with my grief, I thank God for those times, and I relish in it. Then when the middle comes again, and I am waiting for that joy again, I have to trust, I have to grow, I sometimes have to be still and know. Then other times, I have to do all I know to do and then wait again, again, and again. But wow, when the joy comes, it comes so strong, and I value life even greater than I ever have before. Take advice from my experiences, show gratitude for happiness, show joy when life is good. And you have miracles, thank those around you, love them, and then get on your knees and thank God almighty for the breakthrough. The unforeseen breakthrough, the one you didn't think would happen, and it did. The one you thought only happened for others, thank Him, don't wait, do it now even if it's the middle of the week.

How Deep Is Your Love?

Remember moms, when the craze was scrapbooking? I know many still do it, which I love and think it's a beautiful gift for our family to have for life. But it became a competition of who was more creative. Thank God, it wasn't really happening when social media got so big. That could be a tough one for moms who can barely get the birthday card signed for their child.

It became the thing to do, they had every color scrapbook, paper, borders, decoration, and I just wasn't crafty. Now my sister Gina, she was amazing at it, and every tooth that came in or first food eaten was documented in these scrapbooks. I tried, I truly did, and let's just say they had some special things in these books, but it was usually letter's I wrote them from my heart. Writing was my craft, my gift, and so in my children's books, the borders aren't too pretty, the pages aren't designed crafty, but you will find letters in their books that haven't even been taped in but just folded in with the intention of one day I would finish it—Maybe before I become a grandparent.

Well, it hasn't happened yet, but today my son Micah and I were cleaning the after Christmas back to college mess and decided to dig a little deeper in his closet. Have you ever just started with one little thing and ended up in another room, another closet, another drawer, and you become mesmerized by things you act as if you have never seen?

Tucked in the shelf of Micah's closet, we found Caleb's scrapbook. I knew it was there, but I haven't really wanted to go through it. I haven't held on to everything that was Caleb's (if you do, that's ok), except the really special things that meant a lot to him and us. As he pulls down the scrapbook and opens it, I said, "I don't want to look at this today." But a letter fell out, the letter that was never put in correctly with a perfect border and trim. There was probably a reason for that; God knew I needed it to fall out and land in front of my face. I open it with curiosity and begin to read the letter I wrote to him on 1–16–2007, his fourteenth birthday.

I am going to share portions of this letter at the end of this chapter, but it begins with, "You often ask me how deep is the ocean, Mom?" I share of the depth of the ocean and how far and wide it goes, and it's so deep in places we can't see the bottom, and that's how much my love is for you, Caleb. You can't measure the love I have for you. It goes so, so, deep, so far that our eyes can't see the end to it.

I know if you are a parent, you understand this love that I am speaking of; you know the love you have for your child cannot be measured or repaid in money or gifts—it's immeasurable. I think of the love we have for them, and then I think of how much greater His love is for us. I think of the love Mary had for a child that wasn't conceived as the natural mom would conceive, but she trusted and loved this Savior that came to show us the truest of love. She carried a love so deep inside of her and endured so many words of hate spoken behind her back that would consist of judgment against her, and yet she continued on a dark night on a donkey just trying to find a place to rest and give birth to the son of God, the Prince of Peace. There wasn't a midwife waiting, a skilled doctor, a warm bed, a warm blanket, there wasn't an Instagram following to give her advice, prayers, and likes and loves. No, she knew what she was carrying had already changed the core of who she was. She didn't know a love like this could exist, a love that would risk scrutiny and hardship and a love that would one day have to watch her son die for sins he didn't commit so that we could live.

And yet, she trusted this feeling inside of her. It was the feeling of protection and instinct that a mom carries. She wanted to be the best mom she could be. Imagine if you were told you were carrying the Savior of the World? We feel pressure when the doctor says you are carrying a "big baby," but the Savior?

And yet, He came. She endured the pain. She gave birth in a stable with donkey smells and hay for a bed. There wasn't a nurse standing by to ask if she was ready for her epidural, and a team of doctors ready for anything that could transpire. But despite that, she was willing because her love was already so deep. She gave birth to the one whose love for us is greater than what we can imagine. When we quiet ourselves and just think about the story of Mary and Jesus, it blows my mind. Just in the last few days, it has resonated in me so much more than it ever has because I realize she carried our Savior for us. She was responsible for caring for the one that gives us life, hope, forgiveness, and then she had to do the unthinkable that no mom could dream of; she had to give Him up so we could have life?

Mary has always been a hero of mine but now on a new level. I have heard the story of Mary since I was a little child, but something has changed in my heart about this story that has me respecting and admiring her even more. Are you willing to carry and birth something that isn't a child but something God has put in your life, but it isn't easy to carry? It's something you are walking around with, and it's heavy and hard to endure, but you know it is what God would have you do until it's time for the birth of a new thing?

Love is amazing; love is deep, it goes to great depths. Love is when we give out when there is nothing left to give, we lose sleep because we want to know our kids are home safe, we sacrifice our wants so their needs can be met. We love, forgive, and love again. It's a love that doesn't end when they make a mistake, a love that will awaken the next morning to do the same routine over and over again. A love that will walk them through the depths of hell to help them find the light, a love that cannot be measured, and yet as deep as our love is, His is even deeper. But how can it be?

I can hear this conversation Caleb and I had this day in the ocean that I write in a letter to him. I smell the ocean air and feel the salt and sun against my skin, and I see his blonde hair and oversized front teeth and sun-kissed cheeks, and I long to go back to this day and tell him over and over and over again I cannot measure my love for you.

You've often asked me when we are out in the ocean together, "Mom, how deep do you think this water is, and how far does it go?"

My reply was usually, "Oh Caleb; it is really deep. We can't even see the bottom of it, it goes on and on."

That is just a small comparison of my love and the depth of my love for you. I cannot begin to explain the love a parent has for a child, but I know Caleb, my love for you goes deeper than the greatest depths of any ocean, for as you know, at times, the water can change, and it may be deeper at times or more shallow at times, but my love for you never lessens it only becomes deeper, sometimes I don't even know how much I love you until our love is questioned, when you've made a mistake, when you are hurting and disappointed, when you have tears streaming down your cheeks. At these times, the love for you becomes so real because it pains me. I feel as if your heart is beating inside my chest. I feel just a small touch of what Jesus did for us on the cross because my love for you allows me to be stretched. It allows me to dig deep into the things in me that I need to change.

I love you, my birthday boy; the ocean is deep.

Written on 1-16-2017, Caleb's fourteenth birthday

Vacant Spaces

I have this strong sense that comes over me when I see vacant buildings, homes, or parking lots that you know used to be full of cars, people, and now it's empty, the pavement is old, and fragments of the gravel are visible all over. It has seemed to become a place where trash has been emptied, thrown out of a car with the sense of "who cares". Something in the past did matter there. There was a dream and a vision that someone had for that parking lot, for that home, for that business, and now it's vacant, bare, empty, lonely.

I often think one of my callings would be to go and either fix up these places and restore life to them, or knock them down and clean it up, like a fresh start. I just don't have the resources to do it, but hey, if you are reading this book and want to hire me, let me know.

Maybe what was there was only for a season, maybe someone made a bad business decision, or maybe the home that looks so lonely lost the family that lived there, and that family filled it with laughter. Maybe it's empty now because of a divorce or loss of a job. Maybe that building that was a business full of children's toys and clothes had to shut down when the mom experienced the loss of her child, or the parking lot of the church that once was full of people closed their doors because of money, or maybe a mistake that was made that caused the hearts of the people to be wounded. I promise you if you start to look at vacant buildings and parking lots, you will begin to see them so differently.

I imagine what a fresh coat of paint could do. I imagine talking to an investor and seeing a vision come to life, and those who are unemployed able to work in what was once a poverty-stricken town. I imagine a remodel of the home where heartbreak once was, and now the smell of soup on the oven fills the air, laughter echoes off the walls, and pictures of life displayed on the living room walls.

I have a vacant space now in my heart. I have often tried to fill it with other things, maybe a vacation, maybe a new outfit, a fresh coat of paint, maybe a new car. Just being real with you, sometimes I have to try to escape this pain; anything to ease it when it's so strong for a moment is a relief. These vacant spaces mean something was alive before in this space, something was growing and vibrant, and a space I loved to nurture. Now at times, this space feels like a vacuum came and plugged itself in and sucked every bit of life that was left in it. I wish I could go and repair this empty space like the vacant buildings we see that could just use new life. You see, nothing absolutely nothing replaces the loss of someone in our lives, not alcohol, not a pill, another relationship, a home, a car, a vacation. It literally cannot be replaced by anything. What do we do from here? How do I fill this longing and replace it with vibrancy and life?

Well, I know personally I start to dig deeper for more of Jesus. I commit again to realizing that I cannot make this journey without Him or His grace. I am not strong enough. I am too weak in my flesh. I need the vacancy to have help from the surgeon, the Healer of brokenness, the Healer of loss, the Healer of hopelessness. I need thee, Oh, I need thee.

What is it, my friend, that has left you with a vacant space? Is it a wound that seems so deep that it could never be healed, is it a betrayal from someone that has broken trust in your life, and now you question every relationship? Is it a child that you raised and now has seemed to have walked away from you to do their own thing? Maybe a marriage has broken, the one you vowed before God, friends, and family to keep, and now it's shattered, and you don't see how in the world God could ever make anything beautiful and good out of this crushing.

We all go through times where our vision of what we had planted and nurtured seems to have some repairs that need fixed or actually broken completely down and built from the right foundation to begin with. I don't have all the answers, actually not even a teaspoon full, but I can promise you this because I have lived in vacant spaces, and now, I live with a part of my heart vacant that God is able.

I don't know how God has time to fill in all my voids, your voids, and the millions of people all over the world, but that's why He is God, and I am not. I don't have the courage to believe as He does. I have seen Him over and over again do complete miracles that in the human eye, it didn't seem like it was going to happen, it didn't seem like that healing would take place, or that life could be restored. I often can't grasp His goodness, but it is the one for sure thing that will not leave me nor forsake me.

I pray as I see these empty spaces, whether in the natural or inside of someone, that I can be used to bring new life and hope to a desperate and dark situation. I don't have expertise training in it at all. I just know I have seen it before my eyes. I also know that in the time we are living in where we have become so immune to things that go on around us that if we open our eyes just a little more and start to see the beauty in the undone, start to see what someone can be with a little love and hope given, a little extra attention to their details. We can start seeing people restored with hope. We can see depression and anxiety go as we wrap them in a blanket of love and a commitment to see them through, to walk the journey with them.

Maybe we can't fix all the empty homes and buildings like the shows on television do, but we each as a person can find someone who has felt that life has been sucked out of them, and they need hope restored. Who will you look for today that looks like their weekend wasn't full of sunny trips to the beach? Who will you look for at church that you know this service may be their last attempt at hope? I will tell you what this emptiness has done to me? It's made me more aware, more aware of people around me, more aware of the way they look out of their eyes, the way they handle the child at the store. It's made me take time to pray for them, maybe ease somehow something from them if possible. It's not just a Pay It Forward, which I absolutely love and do it a lot and have been a recipient of someone's gift to me, but a lifestyle where we get our heads out of our phone, our selfies, and start to look at people again.

As painful as this is for me, God still wants me on this earth to spread joy and hope and for me to have it also. He wants me to laugh, to live, and to share what He has done for my life. The vacant space is there, oh indeed, I don't need a reminder, but He fills me with peace that pads the space. He fills me with hope that protects the other spaces of my heart. He gives me the strength to grow in the emptiness, to stretch beyond what is comfortable for me, and bring me to a new place. A place where when I drive by the empty, worn down buildings and homes, and I begin to see a little flower coming through the cracks of the old sidewalk, I begin to see kids riding bikes, I begin to see the family who lost their business hanging up a new sign "back and better than ever". I begin to see the car pull up in the driveway with the boxes to unload in the home of their dreams. Hope is in the air; it's in my heart, I just have to see it.

I have to see the bigger picture than this empty space. I have to see beyond the tears and sorrow and see that young lives will be given hope. Someone may not take the pill because they read my story; someone won't be afraid to come and ask for help. My vacancy can be a space that brings healing to someone else. I can't be selfish and keep it safe and empty. No, God is too wise for that. He knows there is too much that came from Caleb's death for it to wither up and die and be empty. Oh no, He is filling it in even as I write. For as I write from a place of brokenness, He is filling it with purpose, something beyond what I thought could ever be, something bigger for you and for me. Hold on. The vacant sign is about to say, "Full to capacity". Are you ready?

Instead of Throwing Something, We Will Just GOLF

I knew immediately when Caleb died; I didn't want to see one more person face this loss, go through this sorrow. I also knew at times I wanted to punch the wall, throw some glass, not at someone but just to get a little anger out. I didn't, though, I truly didn't.

I was immediately thrown into planning the funeral, worried about Mackenzie, Micah, and of course, Matt. I couldn't see beyond the funeral or how we would do life without Caleb.

That is when we had friends that had a vision that our minds couldn't even comprehend at that moment. They knew that Caleb, who was well-loved and was the kind of "loud love," the kind where he let it be known that he loved you, his voice was loud, he echoed even when he walked. The legacy of who he was had to be carried on, and more importantly, we had to be a part of helping to get the word out about the dangers of even just one pill. There are so many people we would need to thank personally, and I pray you know how much we love and appreciate you. Matt's friends, Joe Fitzpatrick, and Ben Houston had the vision immediately after Caleb died. We need to have a golf tournament and call it "Caleb's Cup," they said. At the time, we didn't even know how we could put our shoes on the right feet, but their vision helped to keep us going.

It was only seven months later, September 2016, at our neighborhood Golf Course that Caleb's 1st Annual Golf tournament was hosted, and it was packed and full of people who were hurting with us—those who maybe never even stepped foot on a golf course but wanted to share this time with us. This first one was deep, lots and lots of tears, and of course, my husband did the most incredible tribute to Caleb. Anyone who has seen the videos Matt does to honor someone or just to celebrate someone, knows they don't come without tears. This was a tough one to watch. I remember Matt staying up all night before the tournament working on it. I would see him sobbing as he edited a video in honor of our son that was no longer here. He could have asked a friend to do it, but Matt chose to put every emotion he had into this beautiful video to the song I Really Miss You by BB and CC Winans. The video was so touching that even if you had no idea who Caleb was before, you knew after watching it.

Our hearts were so full of gratitude as we were able to express it after the tournament when everyone gathers to eat and trophies are given to the winners. It was a success, and it was only the beginning. Remember how I shared with you that I don't dream super big for myself, but I can for others? I have no problem dreaming for others, but I realized I am afraid if I dream big and it doesn't happen, it's another disappointment. Does anyone ever feel that way?

So, when they decided to do it the next year, I already felt the fear of "what if it doesn't succeed like last year". I started to feel that maybe people wouldn't want to come again. See, these little fears creep up so easily with really no explanation, but I allowed them to come. The first year was a success. Could it happen again? We were able to give over $15,000 to Honors Academy in Honduras, the school Caleb taught at, and what an honor to give over 17,000 to students at North Paulding High School for students that were pursuing education in performing arts. It was a surreal moment to stand on that stage and look out and remember the days I sat in that audience with Caleb for one thing or another, and now I was again honoring him by giving out scholarships.

You see, once again, we can't bring him back to us, but we can let others know that we believe in them, that there is a team of people behind them praying and supporting their passions. We are here for more than scholarships. We are the people who are praying over you, over your children, their dreams, their fears, and for protection, favor, and the peace that only God can give.

2017 and another tournament is upon us, another success, and another time to celebrate Caleb's life and to celebrate those who have been a part of being a recipient of the funds raised.

We grew again in 2018 and began to have our first women's luncheon when some ladies shared of a vision they had (Veronica and Casey, thank you for thinking when I couldn't), and we called it "A Time for Us". It was a success with over a hundred women there to unite, a time where our differences didn't matter, but simply a time to love one another.

It's 2019, and the vision continued with tournament and luncheon. Our hearts have been so full of gratitude for everyone who has helped to make this happen. These events are not something that someone can do alone. I can never thank everyone enough for being the village we needed to help make this happen.

You see, this isn't something I was dreaming about having one day… it happened out of tragedy. Now when I see the scholarships given out and the faces of hope in the eyes of young people at Christmas or finances given to someone who is struggling, then I can see purpose in our pain.

I cannot imagine just sitting, here day in and day out, and just focusing on my sorrow. As much as I hurt, it would hurt me even more to make it about me.

It's not about me; it's about all of us. A community, a world that is looking for hope in the hopeless, it's looking for something bigger than your identity on social media, it is looking for something that will sustain other than a quick fix. We live in a world that wants immediate gratification, and we don't want to deal with our issues because it takes time, it takes work, literally blood, sweat, and tears. But I will tell you this, we have to deal with them. There are people God puts in your life to help you. Matt and I truly care about you, your family, and what you are facing. Sometimes you just need someone to listen. Sometimes you just need someone to hug you, give advice, pray over you, or even help to give some direction.

Caleb's Cup has a vision to go beyond just the event, a vision to see more lives changed, but more importantly, we want people to remember why we have this event.

We have this event because of a decision—A decision that was fatal and unintended—A decision that has caused great suffering and heartache. A choice that many have maybe made but didn't have the same outcome. It can happen. It can happen to anyone. It's a Just Once, a moment that changes the way we will live our entire life. Caleb's Cup is an event that happened because of a tragedy but an event that can possibly help to save the lives of someone else.

Maybe there is someone contemplating life isn't worth it, and they hear the story of hope given and the joy Caleb brought, and soon they start to feel life well up within themselves. We want to see young people all over the world hear a message of how one life that was full of talent and a bright future is gone because of a pill, but yet hope is given to others because God showed up and gave us the grace to continue to go on. I don't want ever to have what I call "selfish pain". My story needs to be heard not for my glory or attention, but because so many are suffering pain for many reasons, and I want them to know there is hope beyond the grief, hope beyond the screams of sorrow, life beyond the tears.

I Want to Tell You It Won't Rain Again, but I Can't Lie

I would love to give you five steps to overcome, five steps to a new you, five steps to happiness, but I am so sorry it just doesn't work that way. I am sure you, my friend, already know that. I have read every five steps to any type of success, and although some great tips and ideas, life just isn't that easy.

Do you know why it doesn't work that way? Because in-between the first step to the second step, there are hurdles, there are tests, there are life changes that happen, interruptions, and sometimes heartbreaks. Heartbreaks that cannot be fixed ever with any five steps remedy.

I will speak for every parent who is grieving. We wish it were that simple. We would do whatever it takes for this pain to go away. We would exercise 24/7, pray 24/7; we would do whatever it took to be free from this pain. Grief doesn't work that way.

It's a different kind of pain, it's a pain that on the outside may not show the scars, but I promise if you ever look at someone deeply in their eyes that is suffering loss, you will see their eyes are different now. Their eyes hold strength in them and yet, at the same time, weariness. Their eyes hold questions, and many times their eyes may seem to be there, but their thoughts are somewhere so far away.

Caleb's death has taught me to look at people in the eyes, to be more aware of the people around me. To be aware of the stranger that looks sad and maybe smile at them, tell the woman who looks tired she looks pretty today. Maybe stop and dig to the bottom of your purse for some change for the person holding the sign on a cardboard box with writing, "Anything will help, bad luck, homeless." Maybe just maybe, we can be the reason they decide to live. We can't do it all. It takes everyone but changing one life at a time can help to change the world.

Maybe tell the coach (even if your child isn't played much) that you appreciate their time and work that is usually for free, tell the cashier that you hope she has a great day, and wow, what if we actually started promoting someone who isn't an influencer with thousands but maybe the one who is overlooked but trying to make something of themselves. Sometimes I am stuck in a rut of the blahs. I feel since this happened, I often struggle with the thought of Will I ever be happy like I was? The truth is, I won't be. It will be a different kind of happiness; it will be deeply felt when it comes. This morning as I listen to some wonderful things going on in other's lives. I found such joy for them today. I caught myself smiling even while on the phone just listening to their good news. I immediately realized I get so excited for others when their happiness comes but seldom my own now. I thought about what are the times that I am really happy, and it's always when it's something celebrating someone else. A wedding, a birthday, a promotion, a new home, a new car, a baby, and all of these things are celebrated and make me full inside.

But what is it about me that makes me happy for ME? I think I have put myself on the back burner for something that will make me happy because I don't know happiness for myself unless it involves other people and their celebrations. With Caleb's death, a part of me has wanted so much to help others that I forgot what makes me happy, and a lot of that is because of who I am. I don't like to celebrate me, and actually, how do you celebrate the one thing I felt I was good at, and now my son is gone? I feel it sometimes kind of contradicts itself to me. I am being brutally honest with you this morning.

The reason why I am being honest is that I realized my joy and something I am passionate about for ME cannot come until this book is completed. This is my story; this is what has changed every little corner, every inch of my life; everything I once knew has changed. I can't find my own happiness in just "making it". I want to be more than a survivor of grief; I want to excel. I want to know that God Almighty has a purpose for my life beyond the tragedy. I want to have the laughter again that causes the stomach aches. I want the joy that is unspeakable.

Will it rain? Oh yes, indeed, my friend. Actually, it's pouring outside with tornado watches all over the state of Georgia. Will we face sorrow again, will there be days of the "blahs" oh yes indeed, but I will find happiness not just for others but for myself.

I think, to be honest, most of us as parents find our joy comes so much from seeing our children, seeing them grow into young men and women, watching them use their talents and passions. We find our lives become so entwined with theirs that their happiness is our happiness. When they hurt, we ache for them. When they lack, we find a way to help them meet their needs. It's a natural thing for a parent. I know for a fact that as much as we entwine our lives with them, God is even more entwined. After all, He knows the number of hairs on our head. He counts the stars and knows them by name. I often wonder… is He aware of these feelings I often get overwhelmed with? Is He aware of the tears and fears you, my friend, cry and face? Every little detail, every single detail, the good, the bad, the in-betweens He is aware.

The rain comes, sometimes it is just a sprinkle, sometimes it pours, then the rainbow comes, and His promises speak of hope. The hope ignites us again and reminds us this was for a season; the rain had to come so the flowers would bloom, so the grass would be greener, and the heart could heal.

Hormones and Happiness

Whew, this thing they call menopause, peri-menopausal, hormones, hot flashes, racing heart, weight gain, emotional rollercoaster…

Sometimes, I am like God, please no more, isn't what I have faced enough? And now this? I mean, seriously? I know men go through their changes, but this hormonal fluctuation is not for the weak. On top of everything else we go through, we get the kids somewhat raised, and now we feel like an alien is living inside of our bodies.

I know I will hear what to do, and I am doing it and trying it all. I can hear it all, Vitamins, hormone replacement, exercise, no caffeine, on and on. I think I have already tried it all. I haven't had caffeine in quite a while, and that was the one thing I enjoyed daily. Sometimes I will walk by someone who is my age, and I just want to talk to this stranger and ask, "Hey, are you menopausal? Do you feel the way I do, a complete emotional mess?" I just don't know if they are willing to be open like I am. Then sometimes I get a little envious, but only for a moment, when they speak to me of how easy their transition was, and they went through it with flying colors.

I know my poor husband probably feels he is going through it himself. I try not to be moody and quick to react, and I try to want to have the "Honeymoon hunger" like I used to. But I flat out don't like this menopause situation. They should have a place that women can go to daily for confessions of a menopausal woman. It would just be a place we could spew off our feelings and then leave with a smile.

I seriously love laughter and to make people laugh. Caleb was the same way, and now that my children are older, I see it even more in them also. I have a husband who is actually hilarious. We sometimes will just sit and laugh at each other. I just know these transitions we all face in some way, shape, or form are things that can truly shape and mold us into even a better version of ourselves. Does it take work? Oh my gosh, yes, is it a constant decision to make a positive change. Do we ever feel like giving up for the moment? Yes, we do.

I want women to know they can be real with me. I don't need an influencer. I need a friend that just wants to be real. A friend that will say, "I failed on my cleanse today and went and ate a pizza." A friend that will say, "I just want to run away for a moment." A friend that will say, "Yea, sometimes I just don't know what I am doing." I want the friend who doesn't make the perfect decisions all the time and isn't afraid to share their story. I want the friend who is willing to share that they don't feel like themselves and need to talk to someone who can help. I want friends to come to me and share the things they are facing, the things their child is going through. I want to be more than a hormonal wreck. I want friends who can be a mess with me. It's okay not to have it all together. It's okay that I look at Pinterest and get overwhelmed with all the options and shut it down. It's okay that I would love to wear that outfit that my friend is wearing, but my hormones and love for bread has changed that possibility for now. I want you, my friends, to be able to say you need to laugh also. Women, we need real!

One thing I have always taught my kids is to be real, tell me your heart, share your heart, and don't be afraid to let others see it. Sometimes, we are so busy making sure the filter is right that we forget there may be someone looking today for someone who is as real and flawed as they are. That's a friend; that's what the world needs. Not another famous person telling us what to wear and what skincare to use, but someone who lives down the street and is wondering how they can save their marriage, how they can get their son or daughter off of drugs, maybe they are wondering how they can keep up with their friends when they can't pay their mortgage.

Come on, ladies, on top of the hormones we have that start young and continue on for a long time, we have other things we are always trying to fix, trying to make better. There are the inner issues that have maybe left scars on us, the rejections that have caused insecurity, the abuse that has caused fear. I care for you, and I wish I could fix it for all of us, and we could meet at the beach and just laugh, but life is life. Let's give one another a break and laugh together, share with one another, and for goodness sake, let's love on one another's children and not look at them like they are a competition to our own children.

Ok, hormones came on strong today, and it's raining, so Matt may want to stay at work longer. I truly am good; in the midst of all the yuck, I love life. I truly do, and you are loved in all your yuck, and in all your beauty.

He Met Me at a Place Called Pain

As I start to near the end of Just Once, I begin to write with antici-pation, a new hope, and probably, to be honest, my first after death accomplishment for myself.

I was thinking many years ago after I wrote my first book that never got published. Who Hit the Light Switch that the book would be the book of real and raw, and I would never have to face darkness like that again.

Well, here I am in the last chapter of Just Once, and I would love to say the darkness doesn't try to come back. Oh, indeed it does. Why? Because my love for Caleb hasn't lessened, my aching and yearning for Caleb to be here in my presence hasn't stop. I seriously have been to the doctor several times because my heart always aches. The Doctor said it's the 800-pound weight I carry of loss.

My heart beating differently is a constant reminder of what is miss-ing, what has happened in my life, my families' life. I catch myself breathing deeply, inhaling, and exhaling deeper. I catch myself always with my hand on my chest as if it will save me from the heartache.

You see, death and absence don't change the fact that I still say to myself, "I need to call Caleb and tell him," or I think I see him walking through the door with his guitar. Time doesn't erase the longing to smell his skin, hear his voice. What time does is teach you to breathe differently. It teaches you the triggers that, at times, you have to stay away from. It teaches you about those who have never forgotten with you. Time has taught me that my love for Caleb couldn't be measured in his days on earth because it extends beyond his life here and into eternity, where I know I will see him again. Time cannot heal the desire to see him get married, have children, to see his dreams come true to be a musician.

Since Caleb's death, my heart has ached over and over again for friends who have lost their son or daughter, many without any warning, and death has knocked on their door, and their heart forever will beat differently. I see their lives now forever changed and clinging to every bit of hope they can get. I see them struggle as we do. You see, this story isn't just about my loss, my grief, but it's about you, your loss, whether it be death, marriage, or disappointments in life.

This book is to show you His grace is sufficient for all of us, no matter how big or how small. I am here to tell you what I thought was impossible to live through the night of his death, we are here four years later. In many ways, stronger because I can honestly now share with you that there is hope beyond the grave; there is life beyond our pain. There is laugher in the rain. There is light in the darkness of night when the tears flow on your pillow. There will be days, hours, and times where the pain doesn't seem to lift. Oh, my friend, it's so normal, but then you will have days and even longer that you feel grace so over you that you catch yourself smiling, you catch yourself smelling the flowers and the fresh scent of spring, you will find yourself enjoying things you used to enjoy and even new things. No, it won't be the same, but it will have a new presence of hope with each new day, each new experience.

So, to those of you reading this and you haven't lost someone, I would say thank God and give gratitude for that. If you know someone who has lost someone, speak to them about who they lost, speak their name, share memories, don't give advice, just listen. Go sit with them even if no words are spoken, text them that they are on your heart, just don't forget that no matter how many years their heart still aches for them. They long for their lives to be how they were, and yet they know each day brings them closer to seeing them again.

I close with this, my friends. I am here for you. I don't have to know you to pray for you. I care about your hurts, your aching heart, your fears, and I long to share with you about this amazing man called Jesus. He is there for us in our "Just Once Moments of mistakes, our

Just Once longings to hold our child one more time, and He reminds us that because of Him, we can have Hope in Just One touch".

"For I know the plans I have for you," declares the Lord, "plans to prosper you and not to harm you, plans to give you hope and a future."

—Jeremiah 29:11

References

"I'll Be Home for Christmas by Kim Gannon & Walter Kent." 2020. Lyrics Mode.Com. 2020. https://www.lyrics.com/lyric/5047226/Bing+Crosby/I%27ll+Be+Home+for+Christmas.

"I Need Thee Every Hour by Annie S. Hawkins, 1872." 2020. Hymnary.Org. 2020. https://hymnary.org/text/i_need_thee_every_hour_most_gracious_lor.

"It's Just Another New Year's Eve by Maritn Panzer & Barry Manilow, 1977." 2020. Lyrics.Com. 2020. https://www.azlyrics.com/lyrics/barrymanilow/itsjustanothernewyearseve.html.

"Middle." 2020. Merriam-Webster Online Dictionary. Merriam-Webster, Incorporated. 2020. https://www.merriam-webster.com/dictionary/middle.

The Holy Bible: New International Version [NIV]. 1984. Grand Rapids: Zonderman Publishing House. https://www.biblegateway.com/versions/New-International-Version-NIV-Bible/#booklist.

The Holy Bible: The New King James Version [NKJV]. 1999. Nashville, TN: Thomas Nelson, Inc. https://www.biblegateway.com/versions/New-King-James-Version-NKJV-Bible/#booklist.

About the Author

Born and raised in ministry, I had seen and lived through disappointments. Married to Matt Lucas in 1989 and now married for thirty-one years. My dream came true when I became a mom in 1993 to our firstborn, Caleb, and again in 1995 to Sharon Mackenzie, and we felt complete in 1999 to Micah Seth.

CPSIA information can be obtained
at www.ICGtesting.com
Printed in the USA
LVHW081813190121
676904LV00041B/860

9 781647 736262